Love,

regardless

Also by Barbara Kamler

Poetry

Leaving New Jersey
Two Tales of Long Love

Academic books

*Shaping Up Nicely: the formation of schoolgirls and schoolboys in the first
  month of school*
B. Kamler, R. Maclean, J. Reid and A. Simpson

Relocating the Personal: a critical writing pedagogy
B. Kamler

Helping Doctoral Students Write: pedagogies for supervision
B. Kamler and P. Thomson

Writing for Peer-Reviewed Journals: strategies for getting published
P. Thomson and B. Kamler

Detox Your Writing: strategies for doctoral researchers
P. Thomson and B. Kamler

As editor

Something that Happens to Other People: stories of women growing older
S. Feldman, B. Kamler and I. Snyder

*Constructing Gender and Difference: critical research perspectives on early
  childhood*
B. Kamler

Turn-Around Pedagogies: literacy interventions for at-risk students
B. Kamler and B. Comber

Publishing Pedagogies for the Doctorate and Beyond
C. Aitchison, B. Kamler and A. Lee

Poetic memoir

Surviving
B. Kamler-Levine (with Blanka Wise)

LOVE, REGARDLESS

BARBARA KAMLER

HYBRID
PUBLISHERS

Published by Hybrid Publishers

Melbourne Victoria Australia

© Barbara Kamler 2022

www.hybridpublishers.com.au

First published 2022

 A catalogue record for this book is available from the National Library of Australia

ISBN: 9781925736489 (p)
         9781925736496 (e)

Cover design: Marchese Design
Typeset in Adobe Garamond Pro

Contents

for Ruben, Lucy, Jude and Archie
and may love find you all …

Acknowledgments

Thank you to Madwoman Monologues who staged a dramatised version of the poem 'Josh and Ivan'. The monologue *When Josh Met Ivan* was performed by Glenn van Oosterom and directed by Natasha Moszenin in 2017 at the Butterfly Club, Melbourne.

I would also like to acknowledge the Melbourne a cappella group *Soulsong* for including readings of three poems from this collection in their soirées (2018, 2019).

Finally, my deepest gratitude to Jordie Albiston for her astute and always-wise counsel. Jordie lives in these pages through her generous mentoring and inspiring exploration of poetic form. To Tim Blashki for his sensitive reading and insight. And to my husband Greg Levine for his steady hand and unassailable belief in my capacity to create.

*... when two people have loved each other see how it is like a
scar between their bodies, stronger, darker, and proud;
how the black cord makes of them a single fabric
that nothing can tear or mend.*

—Jane Hirshfield

*... You look at me, and I glance at you:
each heart has found its twin—sadness is
somehow divided. Happiness somehow is.*

—Jordie Albiston

Dedication

You sit with me at your dining tables. Remembering. Your words invoke a space between past and present, when your bodies were younger, more flexible, and your dreams not fully formed. I ask, you answer: but soon you listen to one another; your memory calling forth hers, his story elaborating yours. Sometimes you interrupt, complete the other's thought. We move back in time: twenty, thirty, fifty years. Back to other cities, other homes, to a moment, an echo of collision. This moment, no other. The moment when you meet. You laugh as you set time, place, location, and words burst from the selves you inhabited then. The moment when you lean in, when you fall from the balcony, when you feel exhilarated by the promise of what might follow. At the time you may be single, divorced, or just out of school. You present at that conference, agree to that party, the dinner you don't really want to attend. You run for shelter from the rain and he kisses you. Suddenly. In that space of desire and uncertainty, unsure of who you might become or how your histories might mesh, you touch some swirling force, a gravitational field, and an energy pulls you towards one another. Is it confusing? Thrilling? Accidental? You are headed somewhere else but are stopped by this moment. And life will never be the same. It is with gratitude that I tell your stories.

BK 2021

Author's Note

1. The beginning

It is 1999. I am a single mother, a committed academic and an emerging poet, yearning for love and never finding it. Finally I have given up on love—long after the betrayals and crushing disappointment of a fourteen-year marriage, long after a string of never-quite-right flirtations following divorce.

So I am taken aback when Greg appears, as if dropped from the heavens into our mutual friends' home on a Saturday night. I notice him right away—at the fireplace telling stories, at ease within himself, his face open and warm. We are introduced, chat, retreat to other conversations. But there is a spark, a possibility. That pressure in the chest—at once urgent, and afraid.

At subsequent dinners and lunches Greg and I are astonished to discover so much likeness. Both the eldest of three, we grow up on opposite sides of the world, with similar despotic dads, long-suffering protective mums (*you know your father has his ways*) and a strangling set of expectations as first-born. We both marry the wrong one, run away to desert climes, learn to live with years of parental silence and devastating disapproval. Later we send our only sons to the same school in Melbourne, yet never once sight each other—in parking lots or at parent-teacher nights—until now. Aged fifty-two and fifty-four years, long after our boys have flown, our moment, we meet.

In time we take the day off work to celebrate one year together. Enjoy a lavish lunch at a Yarra Valley winery. But I am anxious. Soon we will travel to New Jersey where Greg will be paraded before my family as the 'finally you found him' guy. I have worried how to warn him.

You know, I say, my dad's first question will be: When do you plan to marry? Really, Greg says. Flabbergasted. Are you sure? (seemingly unaware that all our friends have already asked the same question). Well, he says in his deadpan way, what's the answer? There is a pause, a heartbeat. Me: I think the answer is yes. And him: I think yes. Definitely YES.

No rose petals or bended knee, no sky-written message or ring hidden in the soufflé. Just yes. Possibly the least romantic proposal ever. But we are old enough and scarred enough to know what we have found. On August the fifth two thousand and one we wed under the chuppah to *the one* our parents hoped we'd find so many years before.

Still I find it miraculous—this confluence of timing or serendipity that brings us together and keeps us together over the following two decades until now. In all the years before or since I never imagined such ease or compatibility to be possible. Herein lies the kernel of this collection—a desire to celebrate love that surprises and endures over time.

2. The process

Then as now I remain fascinated by long love. And so I set out to meet with couples who have lived and loved together for at least twenty years. As a culture, we are inundated by romantic narratives which dramatise the passionate beginnings of young love and/or detail its devastating endings. But what about couples who survive the years together, remaining committed and true to each other, and to love? What do we know of such stories outside stereotypes of the unimaginative, stale or stuck? These are the stories I explore and celebrate in Love, regardless—delving into the intimacy of connecting as well as negotiating the complications that inevitably arise, and the solidity that ultimately emerges.

Fourteen Australian couples inhabit this volume. They are actual people who live and love, the events they recount really happen, but it is my crafting of that experience—deciding which details to include, foreground or background—which appears here. Yet I present their chronicles as veritable—grounded in the particulars of their lives, which I hope will resonate more broadly with others who have shared long relationships with someone, or wish they had.

The names of each couple have been fictionalised to provide anonymity, but it is a compromised kind of concealment: friends, family, acquaintances, workmates in their worlds will undoubtedly recognise some of them for who they are. But a name change lifts each story an inch above reality and highlights the constructed nature of all narrative accounts.

While each poem had its beginning in a conversation, a unique mode of storytelling emerged—based on interviews but transformed into rhythmic, syllabic verse. It is a hybrid form which taps into my history as a socio-linguist—steeped in the traditions of research interviewing over a thirty-year academic career—and my more recent work as a poet of narrative non-fiction. The impulse towards poetry first occurred in the Holocaust memoir *Surviving*, where I utilised the sociological genre of the 'transcript poem' to capture the words of interviewee Blanka Wise, albeit pared back and economically shaped. My continuing passion for poetry led to my first formal collection, *Leaving New Jersey*, which was published in 2016. In the volume you hold, I opt for the pleasures and constraints of syllabic verse. It is a heady, obsessive business counting syllables—fingers tapping the table 1 2 3 4 5 6 7 8 9 10 11 12, ensuring each line has the same syllable count, reading aloud, adjusting a word, disturbing the text, starting again.

Following the initial interview conversation, I transcribed each couple's words into poems. Words on the page and voices in my head, I tuned into their rhythms of speech, tone of voice, pacing and manner of interacting—who speaks first, longest, more definitely, with what emphasis and attention to detail.

Yet I chose not to adopt the tedium of a Question and Answer schematic, or a verbatim dialogue. These are stories of love, and the telling needs to be pared back and shaped to get to the heart of things.

Syllabics are a powerful container for holding the spoken word so it comes alive on the page. When the banalities of everyday speech are removed—the fillers and hesitancies, the bland verbs, the occasional flat vernacular—it is easier to access the energy and passion of each speaker. And when poetic devices are called on to further enliven that speech through alliteration, refrain and internal rhyme, it creates both illusion and the enhancement of a truth already there.

Most of the poems are formatted vertically, one voice following the next down the page. For others, a horizontal presentation, each turn jostling side by side. As one partner finishes a sequence of thought, the other may amplify, differ, agree or interrupt with their own angle on past and present life together. To distinguish each voice I have further relied on the few keyboard tools available—exclamation marks!, CAPITALS, underlining, *italics,* long dashes—. Thus love is literally visualised from two perspectives; two parts making a whole.

3. The book

This project has been in the making for over four years. In 2017 I began by interviewing a few friends to evaluate how the process might unfold. Not surprisingly, my opening questions were: How did you meet? Where were you? What was happening in your life at that time? From there conversations flowed more organically, as couples recalled their beginnings from the vantage point of later in their lives.

As word spread of my intent, people suggested others who might be willing to meet with me, and so a kind of classic snowballing process emerged. Certainly I found great diversity of experience—of cultural affiliation, gender identity, migration and work in academic, music, business, literary and legal worlds—relationships not simply circumscribed by the boundaries of my own social world. In retrospect, this approach maximised the trust needed for couples to speak their hearts and minds, as I was often a stranger to them. As one gentleman remarked, I don't know you from a bar of soap but I know 'Mandy' well, and if she trusts you, so will I.

Over time, as the stories began to dialogue with one another, new patterns emerged. It was not only the beginnings that couples celebrated, but the enduring. Sustaining love over time was critical. Many complexities were revealed—the crushing pressure of racial or sexual norms, the challenge of chronic illness or disparate histories, the strenuous demands of extended family or geographic distance. Each poem, each story, each couple faces unique trials. They age and change, the unexpected happens, but they move forward, together, regardless.

The result is a surprising and affecting collection as couples revisit the past, having survived and appreciated all that has happened in between. There is no simple secret to longevity in relationships. The stories recounted in these pages yield a variety of perspectives—on laughter, mutual respect, careful listening, stoicism, the tenacity to wait and persevere. Above all, they make real the possibility of mutual care and nourishment over a lifetime, more important than ever in times of pandemic and unprecedented local/global disasters.

Penny and Daniel

Is it love at first sight? Almost. Only hours after they are formally introduced by a mutual friend, Penny and Daniel fall head over heels, literally in love. She is twenty-five, a young lawyer deeply involved in Labor Party politics and he, twenty-three, works in the Justice Department in Brisbane. Their relocation to Melbourne in 1995 to take up new employment and study opportunities marks the beginning of many adventures outside the comfort zone of close family and friends. The line between work and recreation is often blurred as they journey overseas to Canada and beyond. Penny and Daniel savour the planning and pleasure of exploring the world together—just the two of them, days on end. Their careers in law blossom after their return to Melbourne in 2006, Penny as a judicial officer and Daniel as a barrister at the Victorian Bar. They share a passionate commitment to indigenous and refugee rights and work determinedly as advocates for human rights.

Penny

After-work drinks at my firm. It's a casual meeting—
no agenda. We're young committed lawyers discussing
law reform in Queensland. That's romance for you—we love the

law! I'm sitting and Daniel's crouching beside me—bent down
low, unpicking criminal code. The talk's intense and we're
oblivious to the Friday night mayhem around us.

He's cute—round tortoise-shell glasses, double-breasted suit. I'm
decked out in bottle green, huge shoulder pads, pencil-thin skirt—
so nineties. I think Wow there *are* men in the world I can

converse with—interesting, politically-smart men. That's
Daniel. He's kind, well-read and normal. My boyfriend is *not.*
Maybe crazy, maybe obsessed—but seven years of my

life—what a mistake! After the break-up he torches my
car! It's then our mate Mel decides Daniel and I should date.
She's a trainee lawyer at our firm—invites him to join

us for drinks. But word soon gets out. All day colleagues rib me
about this boy I'm about to greet. He's in Reception
my boss says. He's *ugly* Penny. *God! I'm so embarrassed!*

Daniel

You shake my hand then ignore me for the next hour as if
we've never met before. But after three tequilas, it
begins—the most extraordinary weekend of my

life. August twenty-fifth, nineteen ninety-five. We leave with
your colleagues to play pool and land at your boss' house for
a barbecue and bottle of gin—then onward to the

unforgettable Empire Hotel. Two in the morning,
loud music pumping—we escape to the balcony for
our FIRST KISS. And BANG! At that very moment, the lattice

railing collapses and down we go. We fall together.
DOWN DOWN tumbling towards the ground. Saved by the awning
a metre below—Penny's body flopped onto mine. I'm

badly bruised but no broken bones. She doesn't even spill
her beer. What a woman! We're in fits of laughter when the
security guard accosts us for making a racket!

Listen Mate I yell, your balcony is meant to be SAFE!
Back off! Bizarrely he shells out fifty dollars to us
as compensation, says sorry and the revelry goes

on. We hang out at my house all weekend, talking talking
inner-city walking through parks, gardens. Listening to
music. Kissing, more kissing. I'm sure this is meant to be.

Penny

Most mornings we meet for coffee at Café de l'Amour.
It's exciting to share *so much* in common—passion for
social justice, women's rights, indigenous rights, the law.

We really hope to change the world *at least a little*—through
our work. When I fly to country Queensland for a Labor
Party Inquiry, Daniel drives me to the airport. My

brief is to represent the Member for Brisbane—the first
woman in twenty years to meet country seat delegates.
I'm *chuffed*. As I board the plane Daniel hands me a letter.

Don't read it till Roma! I'm intrigued but it slips my mind
as I spend my day inspired by old unionists keeping
the Labor torch alight. His words win my heart. Completely.

Daniel

Penny. As I write I'm feeling very emotional
perhaps because we only had four hours sleep last night.
I can't get you out of my mind. I'm ecstatic, almost

overwhelmed by all I see in you. I believe that the
fundamental part of a person, their presence, is known
and recognised immediately. And the part of you

I have seen has completely disarmed me. It may be trite
to say but your laughter/kisses dominate my life right
now. I admire your work ethic, your engaging way with

people. This is not pointless flattery or inflated
praise. Yet I worry that if I express my feelings, you
may take it the wrong way. I'm not dependent. I'm happy

alone but also enjoy the company of others.
I know what I find attractive and totally see that
in you. To be honest, I've tried to keep women at arm's

length after hurtful experiences in the past. With
you that's futile. We've been together for just fifteen days
yet I'm falling in love with you and don't know what to do!

Penny

I'm junior being shown the ropes by Labor seniors on
State executive, delving into leadership factions
the possibility of a seat some time down the track.

Yet the closer I move to the centre of power the
more disillusioned I become. Daniel gets it—he does
not belong to *any* party, even though his folks are

life members. His mum, president of Labor Women in
nineteen seventy-one, was *done over* by Mal Colston—
who later resigns from Senate for fiddling his travel

entitlements. What a disgrace! I'm nervous meeting Prue
and her partner—strong feminists on the socialist left—
I'm sure they'll find me too conservative. But no need to

worry. They find me normal, even *charming* compared to
previous women in Daniel's life! What's amazing is
I begin to see other worlds through his eyes—possible

pathways forward. We take the plunge! Nineteen ninety-seven
we leave Brisbane—not easy with such strong family ties—
especially your brother, my eight siblings. But *so* right.

Your scholarship to Melbourne Uni, my position as
policy officer for community legal hubs—
one of many adventures ahead, new ways of being.

Daniel

We wed in two thousand and one, our parents' first face-to-
face at the event. Catholic Conservative Mother
and Father meet Activist Lesbian Mums (and Dad)—Prue

left my dad for another woman when I was sixteen.
We're surprised they all get on so well. Fantastic! The day
is simple but deep. Moreton Bay Park under rambling fig

trees. We walk from the pub with fifteen nieces and nephews
trailing—our dear friend Skye is Celebrant. Trestle tables
set in white linen—champagne, piles of prawns, oysters AND a

vegan chocolate cake made by Mum. A few weeks later
we relocate to Toronto. I'm planning to do a
PhD in native title/indigenous land law—

explore an academic career. But I'm quite naive
about what I might learn. Canada is MORE ADVANCED on
First Nations issues, but the answers I need are not there.

Penny

Our true desire is to get away—wander together
live intensely in new places. Your study is a means
to that end. We love our work, love adventure—but there's no

hard line to separate the two. I mean, how many times
has a legal brief arrived last minute—and suddenly
I'm the Brief Widow. Weekend plans *out* the window. Or on

holidays—me in the driver's seat navigating us
around the world—you on your laptop dealing with urgent
matters—like when the Wik decision comes down. But we do

have magic times in remote locations—no internet
no outside contact. Seven days island hopping in the
Galapagos, such astonishing wildlife up close. We're

guided by interpretive naturalists from National
Geographic. Baby seals, a red-footed booby lands
on your shoulder—absolutely *no fear* of humans! What

a thrill. We like the planning—almost as much as being
there. Daniel and his spreadsheets, *ping* in my Dropbox—what's he
done? Just booked flights to Rome! Imagining keeps us alive.

Daniel

I remember our very first excursion. You'd taken
NO vacation for four years—working like a dog as a
lawyer, using your leave to organise Labor party

campaigns. Crazy! Off we fly to Cairns, stay at that dodgy
hostel Floriana. We hire a car, drive to the Atherton Tablelands.
Amazing black cockatoos—singing along at the top

of our lungs to the Indigo Girls, 'Galileo'. *How
long till my soul gets it right. Can any human being
ever reach that kind of light. I call on the resting soul*

of Galileo. King of night vision. King of insight.
I'd love this song emblazoned on a tee shirt—doing what
is RIGHT in the face of establishment opprobrium.

Penny

For us work is not work. It's a fundamental part of
our identity. I'm appointed as a judicial
officer after we return from Canada. Being

back in court is fabulous—the humanity—all the
interaction. But I soon realise our processes
are not well aligned with theories of how people make change

in their lives. The burning question for me is—how do we
transform the court system so it's focused on the *person*
not just the crime. Provide the right level of support at

the right time in a systematic way rather than ad
hoc. I'm inspired by work in the field of therapeutic
jurisprudence—a huge body of research and practice

on how to foster sustainable change to criminal
offending. I've been lucky to connect with outstanding
TJ advocates internationally. For me there are

three essentials—recognition, respect and support. What's
key is *how* we talk to those who offend, include them in
the process—dignity intact. Respect costs nought and leads

to better outcomes for all—behavioural change *and* a
greater willingness to comply with court orders. My hope
is to leave the world somewhat better than when I arrived.

Daniel

I share this desire but my career path is less clear
than yours—certainly not conventional or well-thought out.
The only constant is LOVING YOU and loving the law.

I dislike the divide between academic law and
the *practice* of law. As a barrister I don't favour
undue aggression or conflict for its own sake. I'm more

collaborative, resolution-focused. So native
title claims and land rights work is the perfect niche for me.
Australia is particularly poor addressing

our indigenous past, but there are moments—maybe a
dozen through my professional life when land is returned.
December two thousand and fifteen the Yandruwandha

Yawarrawarrka claim—north-east of South Australia
straddling Queensland—is settled by consent *at last* after
SEVENTEEN YEARS of negotiating. We celebrate

on country out at Cooper Creek—famously connected
to Burke and Wills' expedition. It's the Yandruwandha
Yawarrawarrka tribe who tries to help the explorers—

dying of hunger and thirst—but Burke refuses aid. Such
DISDAIN for aboriginal culture and knowledge! Now
a huge sense of history as hundreds gather under

the big tent in forty degree heat—'dig tree' down the road.
These First Nations peoples finally recognised by the
Federal Court of Australia. Electrifying.

Penny

The stakes are high in the work we do—interacting with
individuals and communities in trauma—long
histories of abuse. We must step outside ourselves to

keep balance. But there is *more time* to nurture when you don't
have kids—walking to work together, meeting up after.
Each day holds the luxury of love and full attention.

Daniel

Many of our friends have children. Initially we think
we will too because that's what you do—but we put it off
and OFF. When we reach our late thirties—just hitting our stride

in our demanding jobs, with no family in Melbourne
to help out—we're dissuaded. I'm not sure when we decide
definitively, but we know it is the correct choice.

Penny

For almost ten years I'm constantly harassed. Why don't you
have kids? You'd be a great mother, don't you like babies? At
times I say I have ovarian cancer—just to shut

people up. I tell Prue I'm infertile as she corners
me continually—I *can't* be alone with her. Not
like my own mum. She's a realist. If you don't want kids, don't.

And don't believe you can bring them back to Queensland because
I'm not babysitting! By then she's in her eighties—with
nine offspring, fifteen grandchildren. She's *done*. We know folks are

judgmental, we have lost friends. There's no language for being
a woman without children. At times I've wondered—will we
have regrets? Not now. We live and love with passion. Blow-ups

on occasion—you in hyper-rational debate mode.
Scoring points, pretending you're not. Me exploding. Then calm.
These things get resolved. Simple. Nothing can pull us apart.

Daniel

We've been in Covid lockdown the past five months, working from
home—Penny upstairs, me down. One fantastic benefit
is overhearing your conversations—the respectful

way you step vulnerable people through the court process—
I'm awed! End of day ritual we cook together. You
as chef, I do prep—cutting chopping measuring while we

debrief on the day. Always we anchor one another.
We've moved cities countries jobs, but this unbreakable cord
allows us to stretch out further and further. Together.

George and Jamie

It is music that brings George and Jamie together. He is twenty-one, she seventeen. Although immediately drawn to each other, their early connection is convoluted and it's not until 1989 that they become a couple. Their relationship is suffused by music—the struggle to establish separate flourishing careers and the joy of making music together. Overcoming traumatic health challenges presents a difficult set of issues. But George and Jamie's marriage in 1999 marks the beginning of more harmonious years—working in the same country, the birth of two adored sons, husband and wife supporting each other with patience and grace. We speak in their Leichardt garden on a summer's day, with cooling chinotto and delicious muffins, two double basses upright in the music room, not far from where we sit.

George   Jamie

it's our destiny to be together from the
beginning—nineteen eighty-six we're playing the
Australian Youth Orchestra season—Jamie's
a complete force of nature—our attraction is
fierce but we both have partners
                    neither of us wants
                    a committed relationship—I don't believe
                    you find young love then fuse forever—it's attract/
                    repel—we're on again off again—don't really
                    unite as an item for at least seven years
we don't allow ourselves—call it directional
dissimilarity—I'm going overseas
you're commencing your VCA course in Melbourne
                    so we MASSIVELY try to avoid each other
it's the right thing to do
                    what I certainly don't
                    need is the complication of loving a man
                    who plays the same instrument—you're a superstar
                    double bass player even then—I know I'm NOT

by virtue of longer study—being older

                no—you're THE bass player of our generation

for goodness sake

                it's a recognised truth—so my

                feminism kicks in—NO NO I can't have this

                love now it will diminish me—I know it sounds

                terrible but true—though the passion is torrid

I travel abroad to study and work for two

years with a world-class orchestra in Amsterdam—

I was born in Holland one of eight so I have

obligations for military service—when

they refuse my deferment for a second time

I exit promptly to begin with Opera

Victoria—that's when we get serious—for

six months we play La Bohéme—great operatic

masterpieces

                we hope to clear each other out

                of our systems—do the full-on fling thing and be

                DONE—but it doesn't work does it—we are SMITTEN

yes absolutely besotted—attracted to

each other in a multiplicity of ways

                but convinced a long term relationship is not

                good for either of us—then you get THAT phone call

I'm told the SSO is auditioning for

a bass in six weeks' time—I down tools completely

to focus—what a moment!—so intimate with

you and practicing the bass continuously

                you play like a dream machine of course and win the

                position—then I leave to study in Paris

the entire question mark of us hanging mid-air—

the next two years are a bit tricky—I visit

you in Paris we're volatile—burning cooling

burning—but on your return to Australia
we move in together
                    although I'm overseas
                    months at a time performing with early music
                    ensembles—my career is BIG in Europe—in
                    Australia I'm just seen as the GIRLFRIEND of
                    the Principal Bass for the Sydney Symphony
this has been one of our biggest predicaments—
you're a magnificent musician yet when you
audition for the orchestra they don't appoint
you—I'm gutted—want to do more— help more—but the
bass section's all male—you challenge their every
idea of what a partner-musician should be
                    well thank God for the Australian Brandenburg—
                    BRILLIANT—I can play full-on seasons followed by
                    superb breaks—and insist on taking the kids on
                    tour—HOW HILARIOUS—feeding Jackson backstage
                    Hold Interval Please! My baby's still on the boob!
                    Those years caring for little people—performing/
                    rehearsing/touring—it's just crazy frenetic
and we survive dreadful crises before the kids
are born—nineteen ninety-four we're busy zipping
around the world—I smash my elbow on the arm
rest of a chair—the ulna nerve is severely
damaged but I play on—can't stop—when disaster
strikes you work even harder right?—a year later
I'm diagnosed with MS—muscle groups shut down
for weeks—months—devastating physical symptoms—
I exercise eight hours a day with two mirrors—
when I see a twitch I zero in on it—turn
around the slightest movement
                    YOU'RE INCREDIBLE
                    raising up an arm—commanding your muscles to

MOVE with a singular focus few people have
Jamie supports me the entire time even when
I try to throw everything I cherish away—
my job our relationship—I'm spiralling down
ready to follow a woman I barely know
to Budapest

it's simply crushing to be told
he'll be wheelchair-bound in months—devastating to
watch his body fighting itself—but I return
overseas to consolidate my position
and support us both if need be—in retrospect
not a smart choice

you're at the bottom of a deep
hole—you fax me in London—The Relationship
is OFF! Leaving for Hungary—I'm like WHAT?—pay
out my contract and race back home to Sydney—NO
WAY this love of ours will finish on a fax!—I
give us six months to get sorted—or we end it

eventually I do come good—so do we—
it's an excruciating process—learning to
manage the symptoms—slowly build up stamina

it's a time of great change in neurology—we're
not cognisant yet of how to rebuild neural
pathways—I believe if they remove your brain and
dissect it they'll find you still have MS but have
created new circuits through sheer tenacity

I'm determined to find a way—regardless of
what the medicos say—I exercise months on
end to bring my body back—how much willpower
or how much good fortune I don't know—yet we still
love each other despite all the catastrophe

for years George is saying Let's get married—I say
No I can't POSSIBLY be a wife—my mum is

truly offended—but one day my fabulous

auntie takes me aside—For God's sake Jamie get

over yourself!—you may not love George FOREVER

but if you last seven good years that's more than most

I propose in the bathroom of our rental house

in Newtown—we're back in the same country—and you

realise

it won't kill me to get married—I

actually WANT to—we plan a big party

with all our loved ones—a proper acknowledgement

of our commitment to each other—perfect thing

to do—it remains the only time that our large

respective clans come together

in the foothills

of the Strathbogie Ranges at my family's

farm—we marry under ancient river red gums—

I remember turning around to see all our

beautiful friends and I'm struck—they're just here for US

—not for a concert or contract obligation—

they love US—what an extraordinary feeling

of community closeness—my deepest sense is

this rite of passage will change our lives forever

and it does—like starting a new conversation—

or a brand new chapter—life moves very quickly

I'm pregnant right away—Jackson comes into our

lives—Harry twenty-two months later—we buy our

first house together and a PRECIOUS double bass

presents itself—I either grab it or it will

disappear but I'm wracked with doubt—what if I can't

regain my playing?—am I still a musician

or not?—this moment is a declaration—we're

setting new markers—wedding/house/kids/instrument

the former Principal Bass says he sold his soul

                              to the devil to acquire this double bass from
                              London—and he offers it to you—an act of
                              faith when you're vulnerable—you're not next in line
that's right—but it's time to stake a claim—not leave life
to chance—of course the cost is astronomical—
we make it work
                              we do—it's perfect because you
                              never really fell in love with your previous
                              instrument did you?—the Italian Bella
my arms are long—she never felt completely right
                              and I'm hankering for her—now she's all MINE—my
                              own Bellissima—she made a fascinating
                              journey from Modena, Italy through Egypt
                              to Tassie then Melbourne—we know she arrives in
                              Van Diemen's Land in eighteen ninety-eight—now we
                              both have STUPENDOUS instruments—we're fortunate
there's always four of us in this relationship—
that's David's* take on things as well—when we perform
a duet at the Gallery of New South Wales
                              he attends—we narrate the story of Chekhov's
                              Romance with a Double Bass—hilarious tale
                              of blighted love—double bass player hopelessly
                              falls for a beautiful princess—it ends badly
a charming tragicomedy—David loves it—
but he says he'd like to write something for us—we
assume for our next concert—*The Witching Hour* by
Elena Kats-Chernin—he surprises us with
several new poems—two double basses in
conversation
                              ABOUT US through the prism of
                              our instruments— intensely personal—how can

———————————
* David Malouf

19

we recite these in public?—we do—interspersed
within Elena's fine music—FASCINATING
often people say You're the powerhouse couple—
it's not real—of course we interconnect
deeply and in everything to do with music—
but we've also had to endure devastating
health calamities—in two thousand eleven
Jamie collapses from extreme vertigo—she
has crushing headaches and shocking double vision

Mal de Debarquement Syndrome is diagnosed—
I can't walk can't talk without stuttering—can't think—
sleep sixteen hours a day and need to retrain my
brain to read—what do these symbols on the page mean?
sometimes I need to breathe into a paper bag
when my mind can't compute—but put me on a stool
with my darling Bella and I can play just play—
George is incredible during this scary time

I organise life as you would for me—buffer
our boys so they're not too disoriented—it's
terrifying—I'm worried sick

I'm perfectly
fine now although it takes a long time—but isn't
it ASTONISHING both of us suffer from these
cataclysmic neurological events—we
don't get normal things like colds!—yet we recover—
I'm sure it has to do with the musical brain
we overcome but we're still filled with doubt in the
creative process—just one disaster on stage
we move from hero to zero—reputations

dissolve LIKE THAT!—enter one bar early—no one
notices but you fall in a hole of despair—
you can't say OH SORRY I meant to play F sharp
the kids were vomiting last night I had no sleep

we're highly exposed it's impossible to hide—
judged on every performance—it's sobering
                    but isn't it DIVINE when we play together?
I adore the way you throw yourself into the
music—your passion intensely audible to
the listener—that's rare—I remember when we
played Haydn with Steven Isserlis—dynamic
cellist—we're electric—audience in rapture—
the power of communicating without words—
a precious space only we inhabit—it's the
preparation that's difficult
                    we need to tread
                    carefully—not offend each other—it's
                    complicated when we're at different levels
                    of fragility and technique or confidence
yes delicate—but we've learned to be each other's
best critic—we've been astoundingly productive
over a long span of time—although it does take
a while to accept your way of helping
                    OH GOD!
                    I remember going to the rehearsal room
                    early in our relationship—you ask me to
                    listen—I say Great let me know when you work it
                    out I'll help you insert the music—you just DIE—
                    how insensitive!—now my greatest joy is to
                    play WITH you—you're technically finer—I'm inspired
                    to take more care—try out new articulations
the boring stuff
                    not at all—you get me to cool
                    down even when I'm one hundred percent—pull back
                    to stay in control—when I sit beside you it's
                    WOW—my internal conversations are MASSIVE
anyone can do that

NO—having technical
language allows artistic language to flourish—
we push to create greatness but know how to put
the critic aside—be empathetic—this is
the challenge it's taken our lifetime to get right
it is EXTRAORDINARY don't you think that we
found each other?—the one certainty is I will
NEVER take you for granted—in the end what's love?
knowing you're completely on my team—throwing our
heads back together to laugh hard and strong and long

Anton and Rachel

In 1974, almost thirty years after their mothers befriend one another, Anton and Rachel meet in Sydney. He is twenty-five, she twenty-two. As the children of Holocaust survivors, they hold one another's history in their hands. They are both quiet speakers, gentle in manner, as we converse at their large mahogany dining table in a room full of colour and texture—their daughter's art work, Judaica and an array of family photographs displayed on the sideboard. Anton is a highly-acclaimed writer, while Rachel, now retired, ran a successful dental practice from home for over three decades. The strength of their bond is tangible, as is their devotion to family—their parents (now deceased), their two children and five young grandchildren.

Anton

During the Holocaust our mothers find themselves
in the same camps—Blechhammer, Peterswaldau. They
become close friends but after the war they part ways—
Batya to Melbourne where Rachel is born, my mum

Mirra remaining in Poland to marry my
dad, Max. When the government finally lets Jews
depart in the mid-fifties, it's on condition
of reunion with family in Israel.

We settle in Kiryat Tiv'on, near Haifa
where my parents have surviving siblings. But war
is always on the horizon, tension high, and
I'm an only child—military service looms.

We relocate to Sydney where my uncle lives.
For years our mothers have the sketchiest contact—
Rosh Hashanah cards, the odd phone call. But when my
mum begins travelling to Israel to see

her sister and brother, she and Batya soon re-
connect. In those days the plane has a stopover
at Essendon. And so they catch up, schmooze over
cake and coffee. Perhaps they have a plan for us.

Rachel

My mum says When you get to Sydney be sure to
ring and pass on our regards. As far as I know
that's all she has in mind. Anton picks up and I
introduce myself. I'm in Sydney with friends, I

want to say hello to your family. He seems
warm, welcoming. What are you doing tonight? What
are your plans? We have none, have only just arrived
from Melbourne. When I say *we* there are four of us

but that doesn't bother Anton. Your motel is
just a few streets away from where I live. Why don't
I bring a friend and show you Sydney by night? Back
then seatbelts are not compulsory so we all

squeeze into his dad's Holden station wagon, three
in front, three in back. That's our first encounter—my
memory is not great but this I recall. We
see each other every single day that week.

Anton

January nineteen seventy-four is when
we meet. Later we speak from public phones—if you
jiggle the cradle just the right way you can talk
for free. Some nights I drive to Circular Quay while

Rachel locates her own booth on Glenhuntly Road.
Our conversations can stretch out to four hours long.
We write. I court her with poetry. On long week-
ends and public holidays Rachel flies to be

with me or I fly to her. In October we
plan to explore Gippsland so I can take photos
for The Australian Encyclopaedia
where I'm the illustrations editor. Batya

strongly objects. Her husband Sol rarely speaks but
on this occasion he says I agree with my
wife. They're unhappy we're staying in motels and
hold conservative views on the ideal partner

for their daughter. Not only am I not ideal—
I'm something of a mystery, respectable
but too unassertive. Imagine the scene—raised
voices back and forth in the volatile Yiddish

way and me seldom taking part. They're not sure what
to make of me. I'm more secular than they'd like
and certainly not religious. I sense I don't
have their imprimatur—why do I want to take

their daughter away? And what are my intentions?
They never actually ask—we take the trip
to Gippsland regardless. Rachel makes fantastic
notes sequencing the photographs. I still have them.

Rachel

When I move to Sydney it causes enormous
upheaval. Mum's not happy—me leaving home for
an unsure fate. She tries to dissuade me. Auntie
too. Why should I go there? Why doesn't he come here?

They're strongly opinionated women who think
Anton's a *luftmensch*—head in the clouds, a man who
won't amount to much. He's certainly *not* the right
one to marry. Years later my auntie becomes

his great advocate once she's learnt how good he is—
how knowledgeable and generous of spirit.
I find a flat in Rose Bay near Anton. For much
of my school-age life I study piano at

the Conservatorium but stop after year
twelve when I gain entrance to university.
I love to play so Anton hires a piano
and is keen to work on his own technical skills.

I sit with him, listen to him practising. His
memory is a phenomenal thing. He is
a natural talent. Our love of music draws
us even closer—a compelling connection.

Anton

We travel to Melbourne for our wedding, held at
the Hilton—over three hundred and thirty guests
mostly from Rachel's side. Her parents organise
every detail. Three years later we move to

Melbourne—and we're lucky. I line up a job at
Macmillan, Rachel establishes her practice
and we purchase this beautiful California
bungalow built in nineteen eighteen with plenty

of space for a surgery. The auction day is
memorable. I feel a tap on my shoulder—
the bank manager whispers You can bid twenty
more if you need to. Those were the days! In due course

Rachel's parents can see I have professional
integrity. I'm writing and getting published
and their daughter is happy. But Batya carries
such strong feelings—any conversation can stride

quickly to 'what they did to us.' She survives the
Holocaust but bitterness colours her sense of
security, her notion of family and
all she holds dear. I know how deeply Rachel is

affected, the talk's incessant. Her dad never
speaks about those times—nor does my mum, though she's more
outgoing, more tolerant in her attitudes.
Thankfully I can always speak openly with

my dad about his experiences through the
war—he's very forthcoming. I have hours and hours
on tape and film—singing Yiddish songs, talking and
telling stories. When Max loses his sight, I'll read

to him every day. Shortly after we move
to Melbourne, my parents put down roots here as well.
They're semi-retired, nothing's holding them back.
They make a comfortable home in Elsternwick

and Mirra resumes work as a bookkeeper at
a local accounting firm. Five months later she
suffers a massive heart attack—the dead of night.
She's just sixty-three. My dad lives to one hundred.

Rachel

It was common for women in Eastern Europe
to become dentists—even in Mum's era. She
recommends the profession—well regarded, with
flexible hours. It not only suits my nature

but fulfils my creativity as well. I
love working with my hands—recreating the shape
and form of teeth missing or deadened by decay.
I carve grooves, incline planes, shape cusps, sculpt surfaces.

Anton

And I sculpt words—like chiselling a block of stone
to find shape and form. I write quickly, my first drafts
with pencil or pen—often in cafés. It's my
habit to number every poem—I do

have an obsessive streak! The opening line can
be slowest to arrive, at other times I race
ahead of myself—not sure of my direction.
Later at the computer, I massage stanzas

rhyme scheme, metrics. But that moment when the current's
running—a matchless excitement as disparate
ideas coalesce—is sublime. It is a
thrill to write a new poem. It never wears off.

Rachel

You can imagine us pursuing our craft at
opposite ends of the house—imposing order
on our respective slices of reality.
We might pass in the corridor—meet up for lunch.

Mum's support enables me to build a thriving
career—none of it possible without her help.
When our daughter is born, Mum is with her five days
a week—morning to evening. Every Friday

she cooks Shabbat dinner for us. My friends are green
with envy. All these years later Anton and I
dote on our five little ones—we're very hands-on.
No greater pleasure than minding grandkids—*part-time*.

Anton

Our grandchildren enrich our lives, enlivening
our Melbourne home. We love the rich tapestry of
comings and goings—old friends from Sydney, cousins
from Israel, my literary galaxy.

Rachel and I give each other space, we like to
do our own thing. I sometimes show her poems for
a first impression, or simply to share. She's an
intelligent reader, it's a rich interplay.

But she doesn't reciprocate by seeking my
opinion of her diagnoses! In recent
years I've enjoyed presenting at festivals in
China, Serbia, Portugal, India—an

integral part of my public life. But without
Rachel, as she doesn't like to travel. What binds
us is a strong affinity for people and
defining our place in the world. We like to laugh

and don't seek confrontation. I've been drawn to her
forever, it seems. She's honest and calm, knows her
mind. Forty-five years she's kept my feet on the ground—
always there, together, as we were at the start.

Janet and Klara

Janet and Klara first encounter one another in Melbourne, 1984, shortly after being rejected by their respective long-term partners. Klara is thirty-eight, on a year-long travel adventure from Germany to Vancouver, Hawaii, Fiji, Melbourne. Janet is thirty-one, deeply involved with her career and community in Melbourne. They reminisce at their dining table on an unseasonably cold, wet morning just before Christmas. Their energy and nodding recognition is contagious as they recall the challenges of long-distance love and Klara's subsequent migration to Australia. Mutual respect for each other's independence and highly productive careers is palpable—Janet in law, Klara in language teaching. Clearly sobered by Janet's recent illness, they are staunch in viewing the future positively. Following the interview for this book, they marry in a surprise ceremony at their beloved home in Point Leo, February 9th, 2019.

Janet

Just as my partner is busily falling in love on her
travels through Russia, Klara's girlfriend of ten years runs off with
their mutual friend! Not the best moment to begin a new

relationship perhaps, but what can go wrong? The frisson is
electric and Klara lives sixteen thousand kilometres
away. Returning home soon—this gorgeous woman from Berlin!

Klara

I'm thinking exactly the same—*Sommerromantik*—perfect.
We don't admit this until much later when we're in deeper
than we had imagined. But we're both well and truly dumped so

we begin to date. Janet invites me to the ballet—to
a friend's beach house in Point Leo—a Christmas party at her
legal practice in Fitzroy. I really don't want to go—I

won't know a soul my English isn't good I have a headache.
I attend anyway—so unusual for me. Then *zing*!
We connect. That party is just Wow—what will happen from here?

Janet

This is our beginning. These first weeks—these days—so exciting
to feel that buzz again. Someone finds me attractive! Yes, we
live on opposite sides of the world with families and jobs

but for now something beautiful is happening. When Klara
returns to Germany—April nineteen eighty-five—she says
Why don't you visit me in Berlin at the end of the year?

We don't wait. I make my first trip to Berlin in July. The
Wall still up—crossing to the East is fascinating. We spend
Klara's six-week summer break predominantly in Europe.

Christmas we travel to Paris, to the Canary Islands.
Klara's eager to experience the Harz Mountains—I know
Goethe loved this craggy terrain but he wasn't forced to ski

there! Imagine me racing downhill BACKWARDS not knowing how
to stop—Klara screaming Keep your skis at right angles! Then my
spectacular CRASH into the fence-line—onlookers clapping

wildly. That's it! We go tobogganing. It's absolutely
divine. Lift to the top, delicious cakes and tea, smooth ride down.
Thankfully she takes pity—doesn't ask me to ski again.

Klara

For the next three years we're commuting. My tenured job at the
Hóchschule is secure—a place similar to Swinburne where I
teach micro and macro economics—English as well. But

we're bursting to make a change—live in the same city at last.
I'm entitled to five years' leave without pay—I ask for *one*
and apply for permanent residence in Australia.

We calculate how many points I need to qualify but
they get it completely wrong—classify my work at college
as Clerical rather than Professional. *Katastrophe!*

Don't forget this is pre-mobile/pre-email/pre-messaging
of any kind—nothing but the telephone for seventy-
five dollars a minute and an echo. You start talking just

as the other person begins Oh sorry—No no you go—
maddening really. We write aerograms EACH day. My pile lives
in a brown leather case, Janet's stashed in an old attaché.

Janet

Dear Klara. Tonight I had a wonderful dinner with my
mum. It's just past midnight so my birthday is officially
over—I'm thirty-four years and one day old. We had snapshots

taken to share with you but the photographer was a bit
drunk. And imagine! This is the very last celebration
either of us will spend apart. I love yoooooooou. Can you hear me?

But Klara doesn't make the points. We're shattered! I recall the
conversation vividly—a powerful marker in the
history of our relationship. Not only is Klara's

residency rejected—they deny her tourist visa
to return to Australia. She's on the phone—indignant
crying. What can I do? I've already organised three months

leave from my legal practice to help Klara pack up her life.
I swing into action—contact the Gay Immigration Task
Force in Sydney. Our next step—approach the Embassy in Bonn.

Klara

You should see us. Dressed to the nines—power suits shoulder pads the
works. We're pumped up—prepare exactly what to say. The waiting-
room is crammed full of old grey dusty-looking people—*mein Gott!*

If these are prospective immigrants surely they've been waiting
here for years! What chance do we possibly have? But Fate is on
our side. A young consul calls my name. She carefully listens.

Janet

We stick to our plan. Ha ha! What are they likely to ask? What's
causing concern? Are they troubled by Klara's frequent travel
back and forth? We've rehearsed our lines. *We understand you're worried*

that Klara may not return to Germany. But she has a
permanent life-long position with an excellent pension
attached. That's not something she's likely to give up now, is it?

Bravo! One week later Klara receives her visa. Now we
work to finalise her application to migrate—gather
airline tickets, letters from friends, cases stuffed with aerograms

Klara

… as proof of our relationship. I stress that while Janet is
happy to support me, I want to work—be independent.
March nineteen eighty-eight I receive a work permit. I'm thrilled

but nothing's ever straightforward. Each time I visit Mutti
in Berlin I need permission to leave Australia—then
surrender my passport on return. But the Immigration

Department moves—my papers are lost. They're stressed. I'm frantic as
my flight leaves soon. I wait. I wait. They phone. *Unglaublich*! They not
only find my passport, they grant me permanent residence!

Janet

We're no longer in limbo and can reside as a couple
in the same city—forever. We were advised it might take
years. Years! When Klara arrives we don't live together at first.

She wants time to establish herself with friends of her own. Soon
she's teaching German at La Trobe, working nights in theatre.
Finds a perfect room in Clifton Hill—close to where I live. Bliss!

Klara

We construct a safety net. Most nights I'm at Janet's, but I'm
not over-reliant on her emotionally. I need
my independence, so does she. Our mothers raised us to be

strong self-sufficient women. Papa died when Mutti was just
thirty. I was four, my sister only one year old. She drummed
it into us. Find a decent profession! Support yourself!

I extend my leave from Berlin—year by year by year until
it runs out. We purchase a home together and I open
my business—the German Language Centre. Settled at last.

Janet

What a life we've built! Our values are absolutely aligned—
our aspirations for the world and for the community
around us. We don't know how couples without fundamental

shared beliefs can sustain long-term relationships. Our only
argument is when Klara's screaming at the tv news and
I can't hear a word being said! She's fiery—confronts issues

head-on. I'm calmer—more considered. Luckily the same things
bring us pleasure—we are united in never taking our
life for granted. When Mum dies she leaves the family home to

my brother and me. Klara and I dialogue endlessly.
People say Buy shares/Invest/Pay off your mortgage—don't go for
real estate on the coast—it won't make money. They don't get us.

Klara

I want to honour Janet's mum. We share a special bond. The
day she dies she asks How do you say I love you in German?
I'm holding her hand. *Liebe dich.* She says it back. *Liebe dich.*

Then closes her eyes and departs in peace. We're certain she'd want
us to do something meaningful. We search for holiday homes
on the Peninsula but find nothing. One night I have a

dreaming/half-waking chat. *Maisie, you left us this wonderful
bequest—please show us what we should do.* The following morning
thunderous rain—we're in Point Leo on the hill of a block

we've seen once before. Suddenly the rain stops—the sky breaks and
two double rainbows appear. Two! It would have been enough for
her to send us one! We purchase the property the next day.

Janet

No water, electricity or gas. Not a stick on it!
Later we discover my family came straight from England
to the goldfields of Ballarat—then settled in Point Leo.

We had no idea! Our new neighbour—a member of the
local Historical Society—learns of a certain
George Cogginbelt who appeared before the Magistrate's Court in

Mornington—drunk and disorderly. Dear old George turns out to
be my great-grandfather! We're blown away. How can it be? My
parents never knew this during their lifetime. We can pinpoint

the block where George and his wife raised thirteen kids. It's confronting—
this force that's drawn us here. I can't express the joy of building/
planting/designing this place we love to share with family

and friends. It's our paradise. A healing home—especially
during my illness. After the diagnosis Klara and
I are devastated but determined. No asking what if/

why me. We do not do that! I have dark moments yes—but we
face them together. Klara is stoic and steady—I can
deal with the cancer because she takes care of everything else.

Klara

I tell Janet If you die on me I'll kill you! We really
understand it does not help to enter the darkness. It does
not! We put our energy into being alive but we're

not silly. We make our wills and plan for anything that might
occur. We adore each other and want no bureaucratic
queries about next of kin. It's time to make our vows public.

Janet

I'm not afraid to die. If that's what happens it's okay. I've
had a brilliant life. I just can't imagine how it could be
any better. I'd love more time, but don't let me linger on

life support. These are the discussions we have. And we decide
to get married—it's the highest statement we can make about
our love. We send invitations to celebrate my birthday

and retirement from the law. Our Point Leo garden is decked
out in white—long marquee, starched linen, sumptuous sit-down feast.
Looks like a wedding … the surprise on our friend's faces as they

arrive is thrilling—we tell them NOTHING. But after dinner
a celebrant invites our dearest to witness the union
of two loving women until death do us part. We say *Yes!*

Miriam and Mathew

In an extraordinary moment of timing or destiny, Miriam and Mathew meet in New York, winter of 1978, while she's studying for her Masters degree. Mathew is twenty-five, Miriam twenty-four. Sixteen months later they marry in an intimate ceremony with Miriam's small Melbourne family present. They love their life in New York—Miriam finds challenging work in publishing, Mathew builds a thriving pharmacy business and their three daughters are born. But after seventeen years the pull of Australia is strong, especially for Miriam, and they return to Melbourne in 1993—facing the challenges of re-connection with a spirited unity. Their pleasure in each other's company is strong, lots of eye contact and knowing smiles as their story unfolds. They sit close, often continuing each other's sentences as they tell of crossing culture, nation and distances that never become an obstacle to their love.

Miriam   Mathew

January tenth nineteen seventy-eight—we
meet on my parents' anniversary—it is
remarkable to connect on the same date they
marry—I arrive in New York only ten days
earlier to begin studies in aesthetics
and take some time out to get myself together
after a debilitating two-year marriage
                    I enter the lobby of her aunt and uncle's
                    apartment in downtown Brooklyn—a frigid cold
                    night two ferocious German Shepherds snarling—as
                    it happens I meet Miriam's parents—just
                    the briefest hello—they're travelling in Europe
                    but stop over to check she's settled in alright
shortly after New Year's Eve I'm invited to
dinner by my father's oldest friends from the Lodz
Ghetto—the Freemans—they escape just before the
liquidation—Dad's dead keen for me to meet them
but it's utterly freezing—I simply *don't* want
to go—no point—who are these people anyway

Emma and Harry reside in the Bronx—at least
an hour's ride by subway—I love Emma—not
only a great doctor but a mother to me
well she eyes me over and proclaims You must meet
my other son Mathew—I'm completely confused—I
know her *only son* Abe is engaged so who should
I meet?—I decline politely but Emma won't
be told—we'll introduce you to Mathew—that's that
next day Abe phones—I met a beautiful girl from
Melbourne—you must take her out—I'm parochial
and seriously need to check the atlas to
find where Australia is located—okay
I'll ask her to lunch—but what does my buddy say?
NO NO she's worth dinner—wow now I am intrigued—
I call her ten times but no answer—wrong number?
it's eleven at night—*eleven*—I'm just back
from theatre—*Golda Meir* played by Anne Bancroft
when the phone rings
I make inane small talk—my friend
Abe gave me your number—howlongareyouhere/how
doyoulikeNewYork/areyoufreethisSaturday
night—LUCKILY you say yes—I call again to
listen to your voice—so refreshing—lilting and
lyrical—unlike anyone I've ever met
actually you phone *every single night*
that week—who is this idiot who keeps calling `
I'm a bit rusty—haven't dated for over
a year what with interning at the pharmacy—
night classes six times a week—not cool to wear my
puffy ski coat—I look fifteen—so I rock up
on a sub zero night in my John Travolta
leather—edge past the menacing security

dogs buzz up—the apartment's tiny sofa draped

in plastic—we flee to Chinatown for pancakes

you throw me that cheesy line

I say if I knew

you were THIS good looking I'd have come earlier

Oh God this guy!—years later I write a poem—

they begin their narrative in Brooklyn's frigid

air—as if taken by surprise the prurient

moon hangs low exhaling soft red-orange across

the bridge to Chinatown—in Café 456

above the cacophony of sizzling plates he

proposes mu shu pancakes—as she watches his

delicate fingers deftly roll them like a joint—

liquorice-coloured bowls simmer with a whisper

of the night—outside the moon hovers patiently

it's such a fantastic evening—we click—I'm hooked

I know I'm in trouble following our first kiss—

that night I can't sleep—*I sense* he's different than

my ex-husband but what if he's *not*—it takes time

to open up my heart again—let my guard down

after three months Miriam leaves Brooklyn to rent

a room uptown so we can date more often—but

we're POOR students—money's tight—she's on a student

visa and isn't allowed to work—on Sundays

I bring her bagels from H&H—small pleasures—

by July I've TOTALLY fallen—she's stylish

beautiful and so warm—it's EASY with us—NO

pressure—she'll only be in New York for one year

he doesn't want to get serious but panics

when I return to Australia in July

will she return—how will the relationship play

itself out—I'm a practical man—New York's my

home my family's here I'm happy—such a long

month waiting for her—I hide a few of her best
sweaters so she must come back—but at the airport
reunited—we *know*

absolutely KNOW—we
find an apartment together on the Hudson
at Devil's Point—the ugliest dwelling ever
but the view is OUT OF THIS WORLD—I propose in
November so we can celebrate with your close
friends visiting from Melbourne—in retrospect I
should've waited for your parents in December

Mum's not impressed because you don't ask for my hand
in marriage—horrified by the gaping hole in
your car floor our hideous apartment décor—
Clearly she announces *loudly*—It takes very
little to make you happy

OH MY GOD it's not
easy—but I learn to tease her—make her laugh—your
dad is less judgemental—a creative man a
dreamer—but he wants us to marry RIGHT away—
we're here NOW why not?—back then I'm oblivious
about distances that separate us—twenty-
five plus hours to fly here—but we're young and selfish
we want to wait until summer when it's warmer

a June wedding at your uncle's house in Scarsdale—
intimate—seventy-five of our dearest come
to celebrate with us—my cousins my mum and
dad return—the Rabbi's a lovely man I won't
ever forget—he says This union is *bashert*—
Destiny—your parents survive the holocaust
put down roots in Melbourne—their only child ventures
to New York—what's the chance you will collide—for life
every day I still think UNBELIEVABLE

47

after the wedding we fly to Colorado

for our special honeymoon—truly I BLOW IT

it isn't great—the first night in Denver we stay

at a charming hotel but Mathew insists we

have to join old college friends for dinner—next day

a stunning drive to Vail but more friends show up—they

sleep in *our room*—who are these strangers anyway

I can't bear to rock the boat—when friends want me to

party I can't say NO—I feel obligated

when we arrive home I finally secure my

Green Card but it's a trial finding work—my first

job—translating obituaries and wedding

notices at the *Yiddish Daily Forward*—lasts

six weeks—I enrol at the Betty Owens School

of Typing hoping to find a new job but I

barely reach forty words per minute—

we need to

find you an interview outfit at Labels For

Less—stunning pants suit and navy blue beret—so

Diane Keaton—so cheap but WOOL and you're out there

pounding the pavement—agency to agency

dissolving in high summer heat—thankfully a

young woman on the Upper East Side takes pity—

sees I can't type but sends me to an appointment

anyway—Doubleday—they worry I'm over-

qualified but I *beg*—desperate for money—

more hurdles to jump—IQ test—third typing-test—

two *more* interviews—*grinding* but when they hire me

I'm ecstatic—love my boss love the job—after

three weeks I'm told Jackie Kennedy Onassis

works on the forty-third floor—she's searching for an

editorial assistant you'd be perfect—

I say no—I'm not ambitious—but interviews

are arranged regardless—I remember walking
into her dark office—cigarette butts smoke lights
out—we speak only briefly—she seems to like me
                    the person most excited is my mother—just
                    beside herself—she's BURSTING with pride bragging to
                    all her friends Guess who MY daughter-in-law works for?
I stay with Jackie for two years as her Reader
writing manuscript reports—it's marvellous but
the environment is too competitive for
me—too corporate
                    Jackie's incredibly kind—
                    when Miriam is unwell she says Don't worry
                    I have a doctor for every bone in your
                    body—she mothers her—it's tender—what luck to
                    fall into this job—VERY affirming for you
it rebuilds my sense of purpose—I *adore* New
York and the life we create there—for *seventeen*
superb years—but I begin to feel torn—worried
my parents are aging—I'm the only child of
holocaust survivors terrified by the thought
of letting them grow old alone—
                    I owe it to
                    Miriam to at least give Australia a
                    chance—for one year—we actually come for a
                    look-and-see—keep everything we own in the States
we pack a few suitcases rent out our home in
White Plains store our furniture
                    I take a partner
                    in business so we can go back any time—
                    Miriam's crystal clear—if I'm not happy there
we *won't* stay—I want *one* year—a gap year—as we
fly into Melbourne I have no notion if we'll
settle—in my mind I think not—but I'm craving

49

real contact for our girls with their grandparents—time
to reunite as a family

                I deeply
                appreciate that your dad never pressures us
                but we're here five minutes and the kids want to stay

they enjoy a different childhood here—not as
strenuous—less pressure/less programming and they
adore their doting grandparents close by

                my folks
                are lovely people but not involved in our lives—
                not present—in Florida with their new partners

here the love is tangible—contact they've missed most
of their young lives—especially our eldest—she
and Dad have their own conversation—creative—
intellectual—we see the influence in
her theatre work

                this would NOT have happened if we
                remained in New York—but the adjustment is HARD
                we arrive in our mid-forties with three kids—NO
                security—I'm nervous—Miriam's also
                under enormous stress—MIDDLED between the needs
                of her husband and parents—feeling pulled each way

I'm aware how much *you* sacrifice—moving from
a place where you know *everyone* to being a
stranger—re-establishing in a new culture

                an English-speaking culture which looks similar
                but certainly is NOT—it takes time to adapt

I soon find terrific work tutoring at the
university—but feel *dislocated*—New
York is unfettered for me—*free*—I can breathe—it's
truly the happiest time of my life with the
little ones and Mathew—here it's complicated
and more insular—New Yorkers are transient

you constantly meet new people—no one lives in
the place where they were born—but the writing is on
the wall—big American chain pharmacies are
expanding like wildfire—we probably need to
sell while we can—find an opportunity here
after five months Mathew decides to buy a health
food business—I have no idea he's even
thinking about it—but it feels simpatico
with his previous career as a pharmacist—
we divest the past—purchase land build a new house
ground ourselves in Melbourne—I often joke with your
folks—we won't stay unless you give us ten healthy
years—AMAZINGLY your mum lives to ninety-one—
my dad to eighty-six—who knew he would carve out
a name for himself as a respected writer
the last years of his life—we're here to witness that
thank goodness
so inspirational for us—for
our daughters who become artists in their own right—
in the end we create HOME on two continents—
two worlds apart—who knows how life would have taken
us if we stayed
we used to talk of returning
to New York once the girls had grown—but FORGET IT
we'd NEVER consider it now—thank God we're HERE—
resilient and strong because we have each other
I don't believe in God—my father often said
he was an atheist quarrelling with God—but
I'm certain He was there the night I met Mathew

Rosie and Saul

Of all the couples in this book, Rosie and Saul are the youngest when they cross paths at Jewish school in Melbourne—Rosie being fourteen, Saul sixteen. They banter together while recalling their innocent beginnings—Saul's frequent visits to Rosie's home for dinner, and later, his unexpected proposal of marriage. But they become analytical as they probe the very different ways their respective families relate. Saul is a highly-regarded, now-retired psychiatrist and Rosie, a skilled, still-practicing psychologist, so it is not surprising they delve into various stresses in the marriage as well as their unbreakable core of respect and commitment. Theirs is a vibrant relationship that has grown and evolved over fifty-two years, enriched by two children, four grandchildren and a wide circle of close friends.

Rosie

Saul lives nearby—he's my sister's friend from school—two years older than
me but four years ahead. Nearly every week he is sitting
at our table for a hearty home-cooked meal because his mum's food

is 'just terrible'. Saul seems to believe I am *dazzled* by him.
Not true. He is a handsome boy—convinced I gaze adoringly
while he drinks at the water taps. Not true. Our first date fizzles out

before it begins. I'm crazy about Shirley Bassey but it's
a total shock when Saul arrives with concert tickets at our door.
I already have other plans. He's not fazed—invites his best friend's

mother instead. *Bizarre!* We begin to see each other when at
Melbourne University, *but it's always confusing*. He wants
to take me out, but says he's broke. Off we go to my savings bank

where he teaches me how to withdraw cash. I'm sure he thinks This is
the girl for me! But strangely—I never know if we're serious.
We don't date anyone else, we often party in a group—have

a fantastic time. *Yet I never know.* Often he says I'm not
good enough for you Rosie, you shouldn't be with me. But I think
I'm blessed. Saul's intelligent, plans to be a doctor. My parents

are pleased I'll be secure. They treat him like a son even before
we're a couple. They feed him, coddle him, clothe him in smart menswear
from our stall at Vic Market because he looks shabby. We love him.

Saul

Rosie's place is one of many I frequent because I don't like
staying at home. My mum and dad are good people but OLD—more like
grandparents than parents. My mother's cooking is UNSPEAKABLE,

boiled chicken EVERY NIGHT! On the one occasion my two
older brothers beg for steak, she burns it to cinders. They never
ask again. Emotionally she rarely engages with us

at any stage. And I am the youngest. When I fall over she
says Get up. If I lament about exam results she says Next
time study. A pragmatic woman to the core—figures I'll grow

up by myself. But I have big responsibilities for her
care after she develops right-sided weakness following a
stroke. I help with dressing, cutting up her food. I'm just ten but there's

nobody else. Dad is frail, my brothers have now grown and gone. So
I spend time with schoolmates—ingratiate myself especially
with the mothers who think Such a nice boy! From a good family!

A *mensch!* Rosie's home is familiar—same Polish background, same hard-
working parents. When I begin to coach her in year eleven
chemistry in her bedroom—door SHUT—our connection starts to grow.

Rosie

In my second year of university we break up for six
months. I do *not* remember why. Total silence—*not a word* from
Saul all that time. Then out of the blue he phones on my twentieth

birthday. Hello he says, totally normal. What are you doing?
At this point he's been banned from our house because my parents believe
his intentions are *not* honourable. I'm on my way to buy

kosher chickens for my mum, so Saul meets me on Balaclava
Road. We're walking, talking when he asks—Rosie will you marry me?
I can't believe my ears. You're joking aren't you? But no. It seems not.

Nothing from him for so long, now a proposal. The only words
I can manage to pronounce—If you are *serious*, I *suppose*
so? And off we go to the butcher shop holding hands! How schmaltzy

is that! As soon as we arrive home Saul shouts Sonia, we're getting
married! Mum's peeling onions for the soup, covers her ears and bursts
out crying! Saul what's wrong with you? You don't *tell* the mother, you *ask*

the father, I'm not crying—it's the onions. At dinner, Saul *asks*.
Dad's chicken soup is spluttered everywhere. You must be nervous, let's
have a whiskey. My dad doesn't drink. Saul throws us all off kilter

but we're okay. We keep the engagement secret until the end
of the academic year. Then Mum places a huge ad in the
Jewish News—a party for over five hundred people. *Insane!*

We don't know a soul. As guests arrive I think they must be from Saul's
side—he thinks they're from mine. We delay marriage till we graduate
so we can support ourselves. I'll be twenty-one, Saul twenty-three.

Saul

It's not until university that I discover just how
ordinary I am. At school I am an enormous fish in
a small pond. I'm prefect, house captain and academically

capable. I run assemblies, welcome guests, give speeches, date the
best-looking girlfriends. Yes, year twelve is truly idyllic for me—
AND extremely unbalanced. When I enter a non-Jewish world

without the comfort and adulation I've known, I flounder. Fail
third year medicine badly because I barely attend. I'm a
gambler but not a good one as I lack the hard resolve required.

I'm going nowhere fast. I'm smart enough to know I must commit
to something—or my life will go to ground. So I anchor myself
with Rosie. I don't plan to propose until I do—on the way

to the chicken shop. But she's a fabulous girl—honest, focused,
caring—with incredible capacity to apply herself
to any task and highly achieve. She may lack some confidence,

worldliness—she's not demanding. I'd be wary if she was. I
NEED to be in charge. An unequal way to begin, but we are
committed to each other, to family. She's my one true hope.

Rosie

We marry in synagogue December eighth, nineteen sixty-eight.
The reception at The Stanmark in St Kilda—a popular
venue at the time, but it has nothing to do with *us*. It's more

a celebration for our Polish parents building their lives in
Australia. *Our* marriage—*their* glory! They don't even allow
us to invite our close friends to the *dinner*—only to supper

after. The most heart-warming part is Saul's speech, organising his
seven nieces and nephews to march into the hall holding up
placards saying—*We Love Auntie Rosie*. We splurge on a two-night

honeymoon suite at the President's Hotel in Queen Street—summon
our friends up to party on the second night. Play a disastrous
drinking game—I'm a hopeless drunk. Saul says I strip and dance on the

table. I have a terrific time but apparently I'm put
to bed in the bath *just in case*. As for our honeymoon—what a
calamity! We only have six days before Saul starts work, but

after one night at Lakes Entrance—eaten alive by bedbugs and
mosquitoes—we head home. We stop at Pakenham so Saul can go
to the races. Then on to Chelsea where two of his mates catch up

to spend the day fishing with Saul. I read my book but it's not a
problem for me. I don't feel excluded, I just fit in. In those
first years of marriage that's what I do—no thought about what *I* want.

I don't disentangle myself from Saul's needs or stand up for my
rights. If I'm ever upset he swoops in to fix the problem—can't
tolerate friction in our lives. He's the fixer, I just keep *schtum*.

Saul

We share a similar Jewish heritage, yet our family
patterns of interaction couldn't be more different. For me
PEACE AT ALL COSTS. I'm desperate to please others, avoid conflict

while you suffer because I seem more concerned with other people's
feelings than yours—which is absolutely CORRECT. It's agony
for me when you behave in ways I PERCEIVE as brash or not polite.

Rosie

You're always wanting to appease—overlook actions that might be
considered a slight or insult—whereas I react strongly and
want to speak out. It's a real problem. Painfully embarrassing

for you. But I certainly don't cope when you prioritise your
parents' needs over mine—fail to take my side. It's a disaster
when they think it's okay to visit our home between five and six—

Saul

the hell hour with our small kids. Rosie wants me to tell them NOT to
arrive at that time—a NIGHTMARE for me, almost impossible.
When I eventually find courage to speak up my mum and

dad take it badly—we don't treat people like THAT in OUR house! Kid
gloves on for everyone! Rosie is more direct—not as fearful
or afraid to express anger because as her dad used to say—

Rosie

I recover quickly—which means no one *ever* listens to me.
My parents are depressed, grieving for family extinguished by
war—for a precious son age six. Killed. Running across the road. The

babysitter doesn't see. What's the remedy? Twins. Eighteen months
later Ethan and I are born. Thereafter my role is *carer*—
always making sure nothing *ever* happens. Always *your brother*.

I become house captain—so what? Win a Commonwealth scholarship—
it's like a death. Because my brother does *not*. I'm the add-on child.
Always taken for granted, all my accomplishments *overlooked*.

Saul

But you carry an ENORMOUS load for your age—working with your
dad at the market every Saturday from five am with
little thanks or appreciation. While I get recognition

far beyond what I earn—NEVER have to assert myself OR fight
to be heard OR struggle to forge an identity. It's given.
You receive FAR less despite all the amazing effort you make.

Rosie

These are the histories we bring to the marriage. I've had to fight
furiously to find myself. You can't imagine the pressure
of merging with such a clan of medicos—all psychiatrists

who idolise Saul as a *guru* who knows *every*thing. It takes
me *years* to grasp that I also am knowing! My psychology
studies expand me in this—exploring how and why I respond

as I do. The most profound change is my understanding of Saul's
behaviour—how often it stems from feeling bad about him*self.*
When I see that small child with little mothering, terrified—told

at age *ten* to attend school and pretend nothing's happened when his
mum has a stroke. When I *comprehend* him I can be different—
no need to get irate when I see him with greater compassion.

Saul

We resolve our differences fairly late in life as I come
to value Rosie's strengths—her enormous capacity to love,
nurture our family at the grass roots level, enable my

role. Despite our many conflicts and conflagrations, we NEVER
wonder whether to proceed with the relationship—NEVER look
elsewhere for something better. No. There's too much shared history here.

Rosie

What's also crucial is your eventual celebration of
me. How you rejoice when I achieve—like my obsession to run
a marathon before turning forty-five. You accommodate

me through months of rigorous training regimes and then applaud my
determination. But you *have* changed over the years—you express
more love, articulate how important I am. There's less anger

less anxiety. And if one of us gets caught in our own angst,
we know how to soothe the eruption. I can say Stop Saul, we need
to talk. This is the real gift of enduring love and deep knowing.

Saul

The glue that binds is not about being soul mates, it's making a
choice to commit absolutely—no matter how we provoke or
aggravate. For fifty-two years we've resided together, fought

together, forgiven together. I love you Rosie so much
MORE than I was capable of as a young man. You hold my heart,
carefully. How could I ever find such grace with anyone else.

Phoebe and Patrick

December 2019. We perch on two single beds in the guest room of a friend's home in Langwarrin, Victoria, just days before Phoebe and Patrick depart for Bali—their worldly belongings reduced to four suitcases and a few boxes still to be sorted. Thirteen years before our interview, they meet online—Phoebe thirty-nine and Patrick forty-two. Several lunches and dinners later, they commit to exploring where their relationship might lead. Tension and sadness is palpable as they recount individual histories of hardship and the many years of trauma and upheaval that shadow their love. Phoebe's diagnosis with a brain tumour is a critical turning point—how do they want to live the rest of their lives? They marry in Tasmania on March 10, 2017, Phoebe's fiftieth birthday. I speak with them a second time on WhatsApp, eight months after their arrival in Bali—keen to hear about 'living the dream' as described by Phoebe. The change in tone of voice and energy is obvious as they excitedly catalogue the dramas of setting up home in a foreign land, with contingency plans should Phoebe's condition worsen. For now their hopes for the future are bright.

Phoebe

I meet Patrick on RSVP two thousand and eight—online
dating is still fairly new. I was married thirteen years and feel

quietly awkward but girlfriends urge me on. I call myself Miss
Rani Girl after one of my two adored Jack Russells. Our first

outing is to Tran Tran in Richmond close to our places of work.
Nerves on edge at first. We click. And following beef luc lac and egg

noodle soup he asks—twinkle in eye—Would you like to meet again?
Yes! Absolutely. More meals like these and so it begins. Our love.

Patrick

I've recently moved from East Gippsland to be with my teenage girl—
Amy's seriously off-track with her fourteen-year-old life. I'm

totally consumed with her welfare but a nurse at work suggests
I visit a dating site. No way! She snaps my pic looking stern

and creates a Patrick Be Good profile. What a joke! Who will I
possibly meet in a virtual universe. Phoebe! Thank God!

But early on I need to tell her my life story—what I've been
through. Take it or Leave it! She must know I am raped by a Christian

Brother—Robert Best—when only eleven. I don't speak out at
the time—no one would. Believe me. It's not until I'm thirty-five

that I finally report to police. Criminal proceedings
are underway in Ballarat. Other victims come forward. I

do too. Who knew I'd endure a tormented decade before I
take the stand—while the Catholic Church spends big on defending Best.

Phoebe

We talk for hours over dinner in St Kilda—I'm terribly
moved as Patrick discloses his childhood distress—this rape plus the

violence at home and dreadful verbal abuse from his drinking
father. Devastating. In all honesty he's withstood turmoil

most of our time together—the trauma of testifying to
the Royal Commission, suing Brother Robert Best—and *losing.*

Constant clashes with Amy. We're spinning around in spirals of
angst—so many cyclones and storms. My heart cracks and floods with it all.

Patrick

You know the hardest part of rape. Is not being able to talk
about it. Worse than the actual event. Legal delays cause

more strain. My County Court hearing lasts three days. First victim up for
trial kills himself. So they ask if I'll stand. I agree but make

a few blunders. Best is found <u>not guilty</u>. On <u>all</u> my charges. I
try to understand why. Yet he pleads <u>guilty</u> to allegations

made by the ten 'boys' who appear after me. Perhaps they use my
case to suss out the tactics of Best's legal team. But I pursue

the Catholic Church in a civil case. And Vivian Waller
represents me. Fantastic advocate for kids. Who've been through <u>this</u>.

At last the Church admits liability! Offers a verbal
<u>and</u> written apology for the abuse committed against

me. Such a <u>huge</u> step towards my recovery. But believe me—the
life crises Phoebe has endured are also traumatic. <u>Massive.</u>

Phoebe

After my father passes away in two thousand and thirteen
my family falls apart. Conflict for years but on the day Dad's

ashes are scattered my youngest sister physically assaults me.
I press charges. I just reach a point where it's *not okay* for her—

for anyone to mistreat me—can't tolerate that behaviour
any longer. The family rift widens/sides taken/no one

speaking to me. *Torture.* I've had low self-esteem most of my life.
Patrick helps me believe in myself—find inner strength. In the end

I drop charges—then this. Doctors find a tumour pressing against
my pituitary gland. Meningioma. *Future unknown.*

I don't reach out to my siblings until recent weeks. *Petrified.*
But Patrick insists so I can leave for Bali in peace. It *is*

healing to reunite—especially with the one dearest to
my heart. So much hurt and *wasted time.* Now I have my sister back.

Patrick

I feel I fail Phoebe following her diagnosis. I link
her to consultations with oncologists but we receive such

wildly conflicting information about possible treatment.
I'm arguing with neurosurgeons, doctors—depart two of my

counselling jobs. <u>Not</u> coping. I feel powerless because I'm a
<u>fixer</u>. I don't procrastinate. Work to get the best solution,

a better prognosis. I can't do it. If she dies from this thing
without life that promotes her happiness—I'll be <u>devastated</u>.

Phoebe

At the time Patrick proposes first thing I ask is Why? We're good
as we are—living *in love*. I never see myself marrying

again. Yet I say it—*Yes*—as long as we *delay*. Romantic?
Not really. But there's too much distress in our lives—his daughter/my

family/the police/the lawyers. My tumour changes it all.
I begin training in Hatha yoga—then teaching weekends and

evenings. Part of the lure of Bali is yoga each morning—at
the beach/on my mat/rain or shine. *Perfect*. I also feel I *would*

like to be married now. It *is* time. A private celebration
with our close friends. That's what we discuss. Until Patrick intervenes.

Patrick

<u>Monday</u>. March sixth. The Test with India on tv and I think
why not wed <u>now</u>? Why are we waiting? Then I spin into action.

<u>Tuesday</u>. Contact celebrant in Tasmania. She informs me
I need Phoebe's divorce certificate in order to marry.

<u>Wednesday</u>. Family Court. They won't issue the decree nisi if
I don't present Phoebe's written consent. Then come the tears. I try

to describe her disease, the need for secrecy—normally they
require thirty days notice. Finally they agree. Ecstatic

I collect Phoebe's medical records, rush to catch the late flight
to Devonport. What a whirl! While my soon-to-be-bride knows <u>nothing</u>.

Phoebe

Zero! I'm travelling around Tasmania—working in sales
for a fashion accessory firm. Wednesday night—painting my nails,

on the phone with Patrick. I hear a knock at the door. It's *him*. I'm
astounded! He says he's hired a luxury yacht to celebrate

my fiftieth on Friday. We'll be picked up from the car park near
the Magistrates Court in Devonport. Seems odd but no alarm bells.

I believe he's planned a special birthday dinner in Melbourne, so
I have bought a fabulous cobalt-blue lace dress. Although he has

turned up tonight, I have a meeting with my main customer in
her boutique. Lo and behold! I spot a stunning cream lace dress. I'm

umming and ahhing—surely I don't need another? I take it
back to show Patrick—he *loves* it. Keep it he says. And why not a

clutch to match? I *am* wondering why he's being so easy. Who
knew I'd chosen *the outfit for my wedding*! Friday morning we

dress to the nines. What do I need for the boat? Your drivers license
he says. I can't imagine why until the celebrant joins us

at the Magistrate's Court to apply for a marriage permit—on
medical grounds. She says Patrick contacted me earlier this

week to say he'd like to marry you. Would you like to marry this
man? I *cannot* stop laughing. We drive up to Mersey Bluff Lighthouse.

An idyllic March day. Janelle officiates—her husband takes
photos—a random guy in hi-viz vest is witness and best man.

Patrick

I hope to make this day just about <u>us</u>. I argue with Amy
who wants to come. I married your mum, I say. And you were at my

second wedding. This one's for me and Phoebe. So much of my life
has been devoted to others. This moment will honour <u>our</u> love,

<u>our</u> union. That night on the ferry back to Melbourne I regale
my new wife with flowers, chocolates, champagne. And a man for life.

Phoebe

When I reflect on what keeps us strong it's sharing the same deeply
held values in life. That time long ago when Patrick says Let's move

off the dating site is incredibly important to me. So
many people play the field, keep their options open. That's not me—

not Patrick. We work hard, value family—our constant. Through all
the ups and downs this belief is the *glue* that binds us together.

Patrick

Bali is our retirement dream. The past eight years we've spent Christmas
at Sanur Beach. We love it there but plan to delay migration

until I turn sixty. When Phoebe's second dog dies I find her
sitting alone. <u>Sobbing</u>. What are we doing? We're tired of city

life. Not happy at work. I see her practising yoga the rest
of her days. I see me cycling in the sun. I see us <u>tranquil</u>.

Phoebe

I say Let's get an appraisal on the house—see what it's worth. I'm
curious. After my divorce I bought this place in Kensington

to suit my two little terriers. Big backyard, lots of space. I'm
shattered putting them down within six weeks of each other. With their

deaths, the soul of the house is *gone*. The assessment isn't great but
we proceed anyway—*with* conditions. The agent represents

us for thirty days *off market*. No auction. No advertising.
Four groups come through—two days later an excellent offer—*so soon*.

We're blown away. Settlement in only *nine weeks*. From that moment
I hit the ground running—shedding cars/bikes/furniture/everything.

Patrick

I want to keep stuff in storage just in case. But Phoebe's steadfast.
No trigger to pave the easy way back. Resigning from our jobs

is a relief. I move from drug counselling into homelessness
counselling a year before. I'm not happy. But my part-time work

 in security at Olympic Park is different—*love* the
concert crowds, the sporting events. They offer twelve months long-service

as back up. Great! My only caveat is Amy. But she's fine—
loving nursing and delighted to be visiting in Bali.

Phoebe

I'm made redundant from the fashion firm I adore—beautiful
family culture, very caring. My next job is utterly

opposite—on the road/on my own/no one cares what I do. I
hate it with a passion so I'm thrilled to quit. I've weighed up all the

options with my tumour—wrapped around the right optical nerve. It
can't be removed *completely* and hasn't impacted my health. *Yet.*

So much can go wrong cutting into the brain. I won't chance it. We've
sold our homes, Amy's grown. There are *no constraints* to tether us here.

Patrick

Sanur, Bali. Every day we pinch ourselves. We are <u>here</u>. Our
plan is to rent <u>not</u> buy. That idea out the window the first

week. We find a villa we love occupied by a woman keen
to return to Australia. She has nine years left on her lease.

Foreigners can't own land in Bali—only leasehold. If we can
negotiate with Kadek to rent his property for longer,

it all will work. In the end we take the villa for <u>twenty-nine</u>
years—within days of arriving. Are we mad? Our visas remain

uncertain, Indonesian law is a labyrinth we really
don't understand—but reliable people are guiding us through.

Phoebe

Those first few weeks are absolutely nerve-wracking, so surreal. In
the notary office—photographed and finger-printed while the

contracts are read aloud in both Indonesian and English. Heads
spinning—have we done the right thing? Are we being ripped off? But we

want to root ourselves to a permanent spot. We've come this far and
the villa's divine. I call it the White House—just needs a good paint,

cosmetic work. We find Widi—builder-plumber-electrician
in one! We're starting to settle. Early on I keep a journal.

Selamat Bali! The flight is perfect, sky clear, our sixty-day
visas stamped. All we've done/sold/given away has come to this. Tears,

nerves, arguments—second-guessing our decision. Over. Slowly
the reality is sinking in—the heat, humidity, smells,

the culture. This place we've been in love with for the last eight years is
now our home. Rapture and relief mingle. We've arrived! Akhirnya!

Patrick

Looking back I can see how stressed I was. In my mind I know we're
leaving, but in my heart I struggle to catch up. Just can't get my

head around it. But no need to stress. You could <u>not</u> write a better
script. The beach is just there—we have brand new motorbikes and endless

landscapes to explore. Phoebe's doing yoga and still feeling well.
Should her trajectory go pear-shaped we have schemes in place. Worst-case

scenario, Phoebe flies to Perth or Jakarta for treatment—
we've found further contacts. Thank goodness that time is yet to arrive.

Phoebe

We're narky with each other the first four or five weeks, like a coke
bottle shaken up then released—*exploding everywhere.* Now we're

in a good groove. How blessed we feel. Our entire lane owned by Kadek
and his clan. Beside us a delightful *warung*—a small local

business and restaurant run by his daughter—so kind to us.
Up the road a homestay—all laid back and family focused. *And*

we've met a *great* network of people—two fantastic women from
when I was furnishing the villa. Covid lockdown has made it

eerily *quiet* here—it's bad for the Balinese. But we *don't*
visit busy markets and it's safe enough to travel around.

So far we've seen Sidemen—spectacular rice fields—Amed in the
northeast for snorkeling. We've made the *perfect* choice here. What troubled

Patrick most was *not* living our best life should something happen to
me. *But we are living the dream!* Sometimes a cliché can come true.

Josh and Ivan

Josh and Ivan meet and fall in love in 1986. At the time Ivan is twenty-seven, in his second year of a residency in anaesthesiology, and Josh is 24, studying for a masters in sociology. After a rapturous and intense eight months, their relationship suddenly shatters. They part for a complicated decade, keeping in touch sporadically, yet their love endures, perhaps even grows as they better understand themselves. A surprise encounter in 1996 is told with great hilarity—but it is a serious catalyst for exploring their differences and an imagined future together. Josh and Ivan marry in 2006 at the British Consulate in Melbourne, to the joy and relief of family and friends. Their generous dinner table and warm hospitality are legendary. They live and work in Melbourne, Josh as a psychologist in private practice and Ivan, a radiologist at a major metropolitan hospital. Both maintain a deep commitment to meditation and the spiritual life.

Josh

My friend Jane begs me to go
to the party. I'm not keen
but there we are—stranded in
a North Melbourne living room
September nineteen eighty-
six—gawking at a handful

of strangers, when suddenly
SUPERMAN flies into our
space, magnetised by my friend's
beauty. Jane *is* beautiful.
He flirts with us, we flirt back.
(*I* flirt back). The music grows

louder and Jane wanders off—
me still mesmerised. Ivan
has flawless skin, boyish yet
masculine. He is smart and

up for sparring. We talk and
talk—it gets late, and later.

We move into the back court-
yard. I'm leaning against the
brick wall, Ivan's hand just
beside my head and he leans
in too. So close to me. I
can *still* feel it—safe, enclosed.

Something's happening here I
know. We're last to leave. And I
have met the man I'll be with
for the rest of my life. My
friend Tom says Not possible
you haven't even come out

properly, yet. But I know
what this is. I know. I don't
have Ivan's number so I
track him down, tell a lie. I'm
at your hospital doing
interviews for my Honours

thesis. It would be nice to
catch up for lunch. Oh yes he
says—and then No I can't. How
embarrassing! I say Fine.
He puts me on hold. Perhaps
he takes a LONG breath. Okay

I can see you at one. We
have lunch. Then it begins—two

weeks of whirlwind romance—drinks
at Mietta's, Luna Park
fun, Comedy Festival,
Brideshead-style picnics on the

Brighton clifftops. Such frisson!
But I'm not sure if he's straight
or gay. My friends say We'll give
him The Treatment. If he's gay
you'll know. They set a table
in the Pioneer Women's

Garden—champagne, caviar,
starched linen cloth. We wear black
dinner suits but I don't tell
Ivan where we're going. When
I take off his blindfold he
GASPS. Suddenly we *both* know.

Ivan

I'm at that party looking
for a girlfriend—maybe wife!
I remember Jane as *the*
most stunning girl there, but soon
perceive the guy beside as
more engaging. Talking with

Josh is electric. He speaks
while I bend myself into
him. His energy is so

alive and mine so forced down.
I feel an explosion in
my core. Later I tell my

roommate Tonight I met an
incredible man—handsome
funny and yes hetero. We have
an intense time in the weeks
and months ahead. I'm bursting
with longing and fright—aching

to honour my heart, scared of
the truth. I'd grown up in a
homophobic family,
gone to a homophobic
school, worked in homophobic
places. My fear is real. It

seems an annihilation
of all I've ever been and
dangerous to everything
I've built in my life. So fear
yes, but also the joy of
finally 'being me.' The

irony is we're highly
incompatible. Josh is
extroverted, but I am
not. Josh is a starter, I'm
an ender. He perceives and
senses, I judge and assess.

The challenge of just being
with each other is immense.
For the past twenty-four years
that difference has been a
gift—fine sandpaper to rub
against! But at this point in

our lives we can't deal with our
ill-matched personalities.
We have no understanding,
no maturity. After
eight months the tensions pull us
right apart. It's soul-rending.

I love Josh, I'm confident
he loves me, but there's so much
we just can't shift—private stuff,
social, historical. Our
situation can only
be read in context of the

times. We come out just as AIDS
begins to devour the gay
community. Gay bars are
opening their shutters—gay
pride is unshackled at last.
But people are dying. Street

magazines announce parties
and memorialise the
dead. It all feels menacing
yet exciting. Our story

too. After our break we go
(alone) overseas. Later

Josh settles in Sydney, me
Melbourne. I buy the house we'll
share together one day. For
ten years we live apart—ten
years is an eternity!
We date other people. I

date women—some of whom I
truly love. And still do love.
Women I might have married
except in the deepest part
of my heart I know what it
is to *really* be in love.

Josh

Imagine! I'm only in
Melbourne for the weekend. Crown
Casino has just opened.
Neon lights flashing, manic
music, that crazy foyer
bulging with bodies, and a

woman painted gold whizzing
by on roller skates. This place
could *not* get any weirder.
Suddenly the crowd parts—as

in a film. And there he is.
Ivan! Metres away from

me. He swore he would never
try Crown, but there he stands. A
decade apart and now face
to face in *this* place. We drink
vodka. Play blackjack. Talk. I
am bursting to tell my friends

in Sydney—You'll never guess
who I met, alone on a
Saturday evening at Crown.
Ivan! How pathetic! He's
back in that old house, still on
his own, afraid to let go

of the past. I'm so over
him! *Really* my Sydney friends
say. But next time I'm in town
Ivan and I connect. We
have dinner and Oh God, I
do love him still! I never

stopped loving him. I bore my
friends stupid talking about
it. During our decade of
separation, he would send
gifts and phone from time to time—
Happy Birthday Joshie! I'm

in the Amazon. Always
I think, if I don't hear he's
married, there's still a chance. Some
weeks after Crown we catch up
for breakfast. We walk along
Milson's Point, rain and mist, one

umbrella between us. Tense.
Ivan's afraid to commit.
I'm in a relationship
with someone else. I can't do
this I finally say. Not
ten more years like this. It's time

to decide. Either we move
in together or we end
it. Days pass. Days upon days
I wait, clinging onto a
precipice until he calls.
Come home he says. And I do.

Ivan

When Josh and I wed in two
thousand and nine, we take our
place in the long history
of others who have loved. We
come from outside to claim our
right. At first we're self-conscious—

that old shame rears its ugly
head but friends sweep us along
with their exuberance—You're
Getting Married!!! Legally
it's not a marriage, but it
is the next best thing. Josh is

a British citizen. At
the Consulate we find strict
guidelines and are informed—The
British government permits
us to perform these civil
unions in Australia

but we are not allowed—and
you are not allowed—to say
anything other than what's
prescribed. *I understand I
am entering into a
legally binding Civil*

*Partnership and declare there
are no impediments to
entering such.* On the day
our clans and kin surprise us
at the Consul's office. His
endorsement touches us *still.*

I want you to know he says,
the British government is
glad to sanction this union.
The legislation carries

absolute bipartisan
support. We're right behind you.

Josh

We have a magnificent
party afterwards. Trailing
down Collins Street to Siglo
Bar for champagne cocktails on
the terrace—a perfect March
evening. We dine at Momo's

with a sumptuous banquet.
Ivan's mum speaks, my dad tries—
but can't stop crying. We make
our vows, exchange rings before
our intimates. Everyone
weeps. When we reflect on our

ten years apart, we concede
it was difficult but not
impossible—and the gift
of finally standing side
by side at the end, knowing
after all this time—*you are*

still the one. That first burning
light was more than our hearts could
hold—just a flash compared to
our life together. They say
love calls you. Ivan and I
were called by love. We answered.

Kerry (and Will)

Kerry's marriage to Will is her third, the one she 'finally got right.' They encounter one another in Cardiff, Wales in 1999, shortly after Kerry has relocated from Australia to work at Cardiff University. At the time Will is divorced and has been on his own for twelve years. They marry in 2001 in two separate ceremonies— one in the UK, one in Australia. They have both now retired, although Kerry continues with consultancy work for a variety of universities. During his working life Will was a builder across South Wales and later set up a successful taxi company, Celtic Cabs. This account is a monologue as Will recently had a stroke and suffers a barrage of continuing health challenges. Previously a great storyteller and raconteur, he has sadly lost that capacity. He remains Kerry's devoted partner—perhaps absent from the page, but central to her life.

Kerry

1.

It's complicated. I'm fifty-five and Will is fifty-nine
when we meet. I have not long arrived in Cardiff to take up
a research chair at the university when we collide.

Literally. I rush into a pub for dinner with a
stack of papers to read and crash into this man-mountain in
the doorway holding a pint of beer, which I spill all over

him. He asks if I'd like a drink! We talk non-stop all night. By
eleven we still haven't eaten. We catch up again the
next day. That's how it begins. Will's *lovely*—standing at the bar

ordering drinks and I think—I like him—I really like the
look of him, there may be something here. And that's within the first
two hours! Saturday he takes me to dinner, Sunday to

lunch, and the next few weeks we constantly date. I have plans to
visit Carl's children in Bournemouth for the weekend—by now *he's*
out of my life but *not* my old step-kids. Will makes the journey

with me as his daughter lives there too. When I fetch him Sunday
I meet his adult children. That night Will asks if I'd like to
stay. Of course I do. And as he often says, I never leave.

2.
The story about Carl is definitely convoluted.
We move to Cardiff in nineteen ninety-nine—but it's never
a brilliant relationship. We first meet in the lift of a

London hotel. Carl comes back to Australia with me, and
eventually we marry—largely I think because I'm
lonely and want the warmth of companionship. The first time he

leaves is absolutely devastating. I return home from
work one day to find his wedding ring, house keys and receipt for
a one-way airfare to London lying on the hall table.

Not a word, not a note. Nothing. When finally he appears
at his daughter's in Bournemouth he phones. Many conversations
later we reconcile—and Carl flies back to Melbourne. In the

meantime I'm so cross I sell both our cars and upgrade to a
snazzy blue sports number, urged on by friends who insist I spoil
myself. Carl is *not* pleased. Our relationship resumes—more or

less peacefully. I'm pleased to accept a plum professorship
at Cardiff University—in part for Carl who's British
and keen to return to Europe. But unbelievably, just

three short months after we arrive—he vanishes. *Again*. This
time a curt note—*I can't stand the misery of this marriage
a minute longer. I'll make no claim on your estate.* A wee

eighteen words after twelve years together. Unforgiveable.
I'm on a spousal visa so the university springs
into action—and I can stay. I never set eyes on the

man again. Mind you I refuse to search for him. Luckily
I can divorce him under Australian law without his
approval. Some time later his daughter confides that he left

her mother four times during a twenty-five year marriage. *Four
times!* He departs/she pursues—hiring detectives to bring him
home each time. Hide and seek indeed! Not a game I choose to play.

3.
Sometimes I think how extraordinary it is I don't find
the man of my heart until mid-life. I survive two pretty
disastrous mistakes but Will is *the one*. Our backgrounds couldn't

be more different—privileged feminist academic
meets solid working-class entrepreneur—yet it works. We laugh
and enjoy like interests—we support one another's goals.

My *first* husband Adam never copes with my insistence on
being me. He's fifteen years older, conservative. When my
Head of School at Sydney University asks me to try

for a lectureship I'm thrilled, but Adam says You can't apply!
You have a baby! It's acceptable to him if I work
part-time—but not in a full-time position. Me becoming

a serious professional woman is alien. My
success in academia doesn't please him either. He's a
senior lecturer when we meet. By the time we part I've

been promoted to associate professor but he's still
on the same rung. I remember walking down the aisle in
St Philips Church on my father's arm thinking—I'm not sure I

should be doing this. It isn't a happy union. We have
horrendous arguments during our twenty years. My working
life is a problem for my second husband Carl as well. On

the surface he's supportive, but has significant trouble
with my achievements. Will's completely opposite. Those first few
weeks I'm afraid to tell him what I actually do in

Cardiff—because of those previous experiences. When
I confess he says Why the hell didn't you just tell me? What
difference does it make? I love you for you. I don't care if

you're sweeping floors or you're the Lord Mayor. I'll never leave you.
Will's a most wonderful partner—he listens, gives sound advice
and respects my decisions. He's always there for me. Bless him.

4.
We have a dramatic period initially. Will has
two massive heart attacks. The first time he refuses to go
to hospital until they find me at university.

We think he's recovering okay—then the second attack!
On Friday he has an ECG, by Monday he's booked in
for a quadruple bypass. Thank goodness. He would have dropped dead

without it. This all occurs during our first year of marriage.
Months later my own body fails. I have a history of
pituitary failure since having kids. I'd been taking

medication in Australia but stopped. The consultant
in Cardiff puts me back on a dose four times what it should be.
Over the weekend I feel odd. Will takes me to Casualty

but they don't find anything. Monday I go to work, give two
introductory lectures which to this day I can't recall.
That night I crash onto the floor frothing at the mouth. I'm in

a coma four days and not responding. The medication
has leeched *all* the potassium and sodium out of my
system. Either they inject me with a high-risk cocktail of

drugs that might kill me—or I end up in a comatose state.
Will must decide. When I regain consciousness he says Do you
know who I am? Such a relaxed man. I say You're my husband.

And do you know my name? I don't have a clue. Don't know I have
children. Don't know anything. But my memory returns a
week later. This could well have been the end of life for us both.

5.

We marry in two thousand and one. First decision is where—
Australia or Wales. Neither of us want to impose an
expensive trip on our families and so we exchange vows

twice. We end up enjoying two completely distinct events.
First is quite a simple, informal Saturday afternoon
affair at a country club outside Cardiff. We carefully

construct the words we want to say. *This wedding ring I give is
the outward sign that there is only one happiness in life—
to love and to be loved. I give you this ring as a token*

of my love and as a symbol of our shared commitment. I
promise to stand by you whatever the future may hold and
to cherish and care for you the whole of our life together.

A student recites *The Owl and the Pussy-Cat*. Will's daughter
reads *A Celtic Blessing*—both her daughters are bridesmaids in sweet
tiny dresses. A month later we fly to Sydney for an

entirely different ceremony. The Minister is
a wonderful man—Henry Lawson poetry, pieces of
Pope, nice things that aren't just Church of England. All my family

are with us—my sister and her husband, nieces, nephews, my
children and their children. The kids enrich our relationship.
My son—always loyal and loving—and Will's two look after

us, worry about us and are great fun. It's stressful when kids
aren't this accepting. Our recent health crises are challenging.
But they'll come, won't they—I'm seventy-seven, Will eighty-two.

His stroke is attended to quickly but the drama is so
relentless—and pneumonia, shingles, heart failure follow.
The wealth of narrative once so much part of him is gone. How

I miss his stories! Certainly he loses concentration
and tires more easily, but our dogs have been life-saving. When
Will is released from hospital, uncertain of who he is

Tiffany settles in his lap—to watch over him. He strokes
her continuously. A year later Tommy joins us—our
second Bichon Frise. Will talks to the puppies as though they are

children, calming and restorative. Each night they race up to greet him as he alights from the stair-lift. They have brought him back. And the promise of love—reassuring and certain—endures.

Anna and Marco

Anna and Marco become acquainted in 1996, working as radical advocates within the Brisbane gay scene. Anna is twenty-eight and Marco thirty-four. Over time their friendship evolves as they engage in intense personal development work and interrogate their respective histories and life decisions. But 2005 marks a surprising new phase, as they enter a loving heterosexual partnership and subsequently raise their daughter and son together. We meet in the garden of their charming Bed & Breakfast, where they have created a haven for guests with style and panache. Their stories intermingle with generous platters of Marco's pizza and other homemade delights, as they share the drama, disjunctions and eventual harmony of their union. Anna and Marco marry in the sanctuary of their garden in October 2016, twenty years after they first meet.

Anna

Marco and I are travelling the world living here and
there—a London decade for him—three years in Oxford for
me. But we arrive in Brisbane at exactly the same
time. It is summer nineteen ninety-six. Both of us gay

with long-term loving partners. I work with Lenny at this
fabulous nightclub in the Valley. You *must* meet my boy
he says—my *life* and *joy*. How incredible! First time I
see Marco I am transfixed. Something about his being

radiates. Is it serendipity or fate—finding
him on World AIDS Day at the Moray Café? I tear home
to share with my girlfriend—completely out of my mind. Oh
my God, if I were not gay I could not decline this man!

Marco

I love London but Lenny's homesick—he wants to return
to Australia. NO WAY but he insists. Fast forward
two years and we're running the New Farm Café. It is an
iconic gay hub, hip-hop and happening. Anna and

I are militant gays. Out there organising epic
gigs—the annual Pride March, incredible concerts—we're
righteous. Quickly we become great friends. As it happens, both
our relationships rupture in sync. We endeavour to

support each other through the ordeal. Anna's in distress
but one day she waltzes into the café to announce
she has two life-choices: become an actor or have a
child. UNBELIEVABLE! When NIDA rejects her, she asks

me to a romantic dinner—reveals her request. Will
you be *my donor* Marco? I'm completely stunned. Why now
at the ripe old age of thirty-one? In reality
I've always loved kids. Without over-thinking, I agree.

Anna

I need to be sure Marco's not HIV positive
so we both have tests, but the results take forever. I'm
feeling desperate, edgy, waiting waiting waiting. Just
before Christmas I say *Stuff it!* Come over *now* Marco.

I'm ovulating! He's working out at the gym—cycles
fifteen kilometres with a Red Rooster chook and a
bottle of red. A few glasses later I give him the
nod. He's in the bathroom when a deafening display of

fireworks explodes over Southbank. So close to my home. What
an omen! He swaddles the specimen—sweet and safe in
a jar—then asks Should I stay? I send him off with a kiss
but know right away. The miracle inside that is Tom.

Marco

Used and abused she sends me away—calls next day to say
she's conceived. I can't believe my ears! But we do indeed
have a baby. Every day of his young life Tom sleeps
beneath the counter at my café. The customers dote

on him. When I sell up and relocate to Byron Bay
Anna tells me I am elusive, reclusive. Truth is
I am in trouble. My lifestyle's unsafe. I'm into drugs
and my lawsuit against my ex-partner is killing me—

crippling legal fees. The night before I'm due to appear
in court, Anna phones DO NOT GO Marco! Do not do this!
Take responsibility for this drama of yours. I
hang up. She calls FIVE more times—demanding I examine

my actions. I toss and turn in turmoil because her words
sting. Anna's right. I've made dangerous decisions that have
led me here. My pulse is palpitating—I feel myself
sink into a dark abyss. I must act. At midnight I

contact my barrister, cancel my court appearance and
register for a course Anna begs me to try. Doing
emotional work is the LAST thing on earth I want right
now. But somehow it shines a much-needed light on my life.

Anna

Marco minds Tom so I might attend a two-week human
potential workshop. It's harrowing surveying old hurts—
unresolved feelings about my adoption—exiled as
a girl to High Church Boarding School. And a revelation:

I am supposed to be with Marco! I try to explain
the choice I made to love women so early in life—fuelled
by my anguish with men. It's totally a lie! Yes, I've
been damaged, searching for succour wherever I could. But

Marco is incredulous—and resists every word.
You are *crazy* he shouts. I am a *gay* man—this is who
I am! Do your development courses but please leave me
alone! It takes quite some time to resolve. I have no doubts.

Marco

One weekend Anna and I attend the course together.
An EXTRAORDINARY thing happens! Saturday night
her mum phones—Tom has a forty-two degree fever. She
repudiates our trust in holistic medicine and

exhorts us to take Tom to Emergency NOW! We call
our homeopath from the car. He assures us all will
be well. Tom has come into this world for YOU, he says. All
you need do is love him—take him home. I hold my boy close

through the night. By morning his fever's COMPLETELY gone. He's
bright and active. We're ecstatic! That's the first time Anna
and I share the same bed, little Tom snuggled between us.
We return to the course Sunday—so much opens up for

me at a deeper level. I grasp how cruel patterns in
my family fashioned my sexuality—all the
merciless bullying, how shut down I had become. It
feels like pulling pins from my heart. But as I unravel

the past it's like My God! I AM supposed to be with this
woman. I've known love in my male relationships, I don't
deny. But with Anna it's different—I'm connected.
Complete. I've never felt more secure before in my life.

Anna

When we come together as a couple I'm thirty-nine,
Marco forty-one. It's challenging—we lose friends in the
gay community, our mothers are dubious. But how
rousing to rediscover ourselves and each other—give

birth to our beloved second child Alexandra in
two thousand and nine. Work-wise we're unsettled, somewhat bored.
We establish a cleaning business—bread and butter—
but we're hoping for more. One day on Facebook, a notice

flashes. *B&B For Sale. Owners must sell! Price reduced by $100,000*. We call the agent, make
an appointment. It's wrecked—a run-down ruin. We *adore*
it. Right before our eyes we can see what the future holds.

Marco

We are short on money so make an offer subject to
selling our home in Maroochydore. Two weeks later the
vendor suddenly DIES! His grieving widow freaks out and
accepts a cash offer from somebody else—we are stuffed!

If we don't make our tender unconditional within
forty-eight hours, we forfeit the property and LOSE
our deposit. I spin out completely until Anna
sets my head straight. We decide to take the risk. Thankfully

the planets line up. Our broker lends us the funds, our real
estate agent moves into higher gear—finds a buyer
for our house. So many balls rolling but one certainty—
this place will soon be ours—a haven to share with others.

Anna

Our vision—design a space where guests can sink into a
genuine experience of care, be themselves. We are
dynamic in what we offer—delectable food, wine
and coffee, rich inside, lush outside. My own childhood was

spent in the Highlands of New Guinea—regal tribal dress,
tropical fruits, exotic plants—it's part of me! I *love*
fabrics, *love* colour, *love* texture. Look around. You can see
abundance in the jumble of objects, semi-precious

stones, furnishings and rugs. My ideas flourish when I
collaborate with Marco, like this Rajasthan door we've
formed into our bedhead. After a trip to Sicily
we fashion this Italian-inspired mural—moulding

lemons and cacti out of cornflour and silicon,
lacquering cascades of plastic grapes lusciously purple.
We're inventive, source from op shops, building sites. With more cash
to splash, I'd make it even more enticing. Paradise!

Marco

It's the intention and ardour that create excitement.
Anna is fearless. Unbound by customs or concerns re
what looks right. NONE of that! Our garden is an extension
of the same delight. Such a MESS when we inherit it—

we see a tree here, a mound of grass there, try things out. And
slowly it evolves—organically. I grew up in
New Zealand gardening with my dad. I have always loved
this connection to the earth—the wonder of plants and how

they grow. The food we serve is inspired by this energy—
fresh ingredients combined with care. I cook with passion
for guests to partake—warm focaccia, garlic prawns, plates
of tomatoes, artichokes, haloumi—a work of love.

Anna

We have exquisite furniture in the yard. I'm crazy
about this mosaic table—vintage tiles conveyed from
the Amalfi Coast in our hand luggage! We *knew* it would
be a platform where stories are told. My greatest pleasure

is others' pleasure. This is our private dwelling, yet we
are energised sharing it with our guests. Strangers arrive
and we embrace them—they keep coming back. Some have returned
eighteen times! It's the food, the look, the taste, the sensation

they appreciate—a unique space for them to heal. We
are open about our life experience so they can
be open about theirs. Last summer we married in our
Eden, blessed by those we love. Exchanging vows before our

two children is a thing too great to explain. I want them
to understand I'll love Marco until I die. We have
encountered so much change, resistance, pain—yet I've *never*
had any doubts about us. It's so potent when you *know* …

Jack and Katie

An academic symposium in Newcastle is where Jack and Katie first connect in 2000: he is forty-six, she thirty-three. Right from the start, their shared passion for Aboriginal rights and history is deeply entwined with their love for one another. Having survived unsuccessful first marriages, neither is keen to rush into romance, but the momentum is not theirs to choose. The growth of their love and their family of three boys parallel the growth of their careers. Currently they are co-directors of the Purai Global Indigenous History Centre, bringing together researchers from around the world who work on race/colonial histories. 'Purai' is an Awabakal word meaning 'the earth, the world'. Jack and Katie's dramatic experiences overseas are many and they survive astonishing upheavals, both in Australia and away. Yet as we meet via Skype during the Covid 19 lockdown, they are buoyant in telling their story, interspersed as it is with mutual raucous laughter.

Jack   Katie

a diploma course at Newcastle leads to a
BA then a PhD—I'm compiling a
family history of my grandfather—a
prominent Aboriginal activist—we
have letters photographs but I need state archives
local libraries research expertise—I'm at
a conference on Eugenics and Katie's there—
what an excellent fluke of timing—we connect
at once—

                    I am brand new to academia
                    complete my PhD in ninety-eight while in
                    hiding with my baby then to Adelaide to
                    work at Flinders University this is my
                    VERY FIRST conference I notice Jack straight off
                    as everyone else seems to be white his ringlets
                    glossy brown glorious and those lovely green eyes
I'm feeling free and easy—recently released
from an unhappy marriage of thirteen years—my

wife and I share little in common—in time I
realise this can't be my life forever—truth
is I'm okay on my own—work's engrossing—I
live from week to week quite content

           and I'm OFF MEN

           ENTIRELY my marriage an absolute nightmare
           such an extreme experience *love is not good*
           for you so when girlfriends try to set me up I
           have just one question Is he a happy person?
           I need optimism a positive outlook
           or forget it! of course there is no one like that
I have a date for the conference dinner but
bump into Katie outside the hall

           NO NO NO

           it isn't like that I WANT to talk to you I'm
           grinning at you all night Hi I'm hanging out for
           a cigarette (breathless) you follow me out we
           chat chat chat *talk's intense* the last day you ask me
           to join in for drinks and dinner with a group of
           friends *ooooh* I have a plane to catch we swap emails

Dear Katie. It was great to meet up with you at
Newcastle. I'm coming to Adelaide for the
Australian Historical Society
Conference. Love to continue a yarn over
a few beers on the early Aboriginal
political movement. I'm passionate about
my research on my grandfather—my Holy Grail
for the past seven years yet virtually kept
under wraps. All will be revealed next week! Cheers J

           I'm hoping for some kind of 'date' to work my wiles
           on Jack but can't find a babysitter so I
           invite him home so untactful but my little
           fella Ganur likes him immediately when

he loses his lego car at dusk Jack calms his
crying tantrum Don't worry mate I'll help you find
it first thing tomorrow morning I think *what?* Are
you sleeping here tonight? MY GOD HE DOES LIKE ME!

Dearest Katie. Can you cope with a long distance
relationship? I certainly hope so. I have
no hesitation …

it's perfect *neither* of us
in a great hurry to get entangled again
indigenous research has just taken off—my
position is full-on and Katie's extremely
busy firing up her career—we click from the
get-go—up all night talking Aboriginal
politics from the nineteen twenties and thirties—
day after day consumed with this history—our
obsession—we adore reading—spend countless hours
perusing second-hand book shops—wandering—then
coming together to haul home wheelbarrows of
mighty text

that fabulous shop at The Entrance
I recall it vividly you and Ganur up
the road for a couple of milkshakes and when you
return I'm sprawled out on the floor in the back room
surrounded by PILES and PILES of books and you shout
Oh I love your mother Ganur I LOVE YOUR MUM!

Katie facilitates my invitation as
Visiting Fellow at Flinders two thousand and
one—I tell Newcastle Look I've found real love I'm
resigning—the Dean calls Don't do anything rash!—
Take six months study leave finish your PhD
see how life goes—I set myself up in a space
at the back of Katie's place in Seacliff with all
my books and papers

no no it was my OFFICE
and you COMPLETELY take it over I have to
move *to a tiny corner of the living room*
my focus is publishing from my PhD
on my great-grandmother an employer of young
Aboriginal domestic servants and an
activist against the removal of children
from indigenous homes my PhD becomes
a published book *in fact it's a three-baby book*
Ganur being born in the midst of the research
and Kaiyu during its revision then Kirrin
to see it finalised and then a new volume
'White Women in Aboriginal History'
this is my idea of nirvana—mornings
I drive Katie to uni/walk Ganur to school/
write for five hours/break for lunch at the Seacliff Pub/
enjoy a swim and sunbake—I draft the entire
PhD in six months

        you're THE most efficient
        worker imaginable such a test of our
        affinity I'm such a slow writer UNFAIR!
lo and behold at the end of that time Katie's
pregnant—I'm now forty-seven she's thirty-four—
I'm definitely quitting now—I have offers
from Flinders but Newcastle won't let me go—I've
been highly successful netting big grant dollars
so they propose a research-only position—
fantastic news!—but Katie's pregnancy is tense
        we have worrying scans I tumble down stairs at
        work and sprain my ankle *labour is hideous*
        Kaiyu's ABSOLUTELY ENORMOUS but such an
        adorable baby so easy to care for

beautiful with a massive mop of thick dark curls
we think let's have another one!

          when I return

          to work pregnant YET AGAIN colleagues look askance

          I say Hey what can I do it was Jack's birthday

Kirrin's birth is extraordinary—Katie
seems absolutely fine so they send me home but
you start haemorrhaging so severely doctors
think you won't survive—I race back to hospital
completely traumatised

          thanks to multiple blood

          transfusions I'm still HERE but Kirrin's a clingy

          fella if I don't hold him he constantly SCREAMS

          it has to be me but what an ANGEL gazing

          at me with such rapturous love Jack has no chance

two thousand and five we're off to America—
I win a large grant to explore political
connections between African American
and Aboriginal cultures as a Fellow
at Boston University—it's unsettling
for Katie—she's never been overseas before

          Kirrin's ten months Kaiyu two years Ganur nine I'm

          stressed out still on maternity leave but arrange

          my FIRST SABBATICAL to research the placement

          of indigenous girls in domestic service

you could produce a film on all our adventures

          we're young and naïve about the academic

          world overseas we believe Boston will take care

          of us and provide ALL our accommodation

they are astounded we've booked a hotel for one
night only—they have no place for us to stay *and*
it's graduation time *and* the entire city

is booked out—not a room in sight—thank heavens for
the Covered Wagon—our double-seated stroller

> SAVES US! two-year-old on the roof/baby ensconced/
> luggage underneath/tramping the streets of Boston
> *like homeless folk* completely jetlagged TERRIFIED

hallelujah! we discover a small guest house—
Rachel the proprietor offers us a room
but she owns a property in Cambridge where her
daughter lives—if we hit it off we can stay—beers
and barbie in the backyard we're in!—fabulous
family—we're close with Rachel even today—
she arranges great acting classes for Ganur

> turns out he loves drama takes a *lead* role we ask
> Who's your character? *Oh some stupid Christian bloke* …

FREDERICK DOUGLASS! Abolitionist hero!
we're blown away

> Ganur totally steals the show—
> the next ten months we zigzag across the country
> for our research *absolutely clueless about*
> *US geography* I'm searching at Harvard's
> Widener Library and the US National
> Archives in Washington and San Francisco for
> material on Native American girls

flying is an absolute nightmare for us post-
nine-eleven—we get right up to the front of
the line—officials drag me out to inspect our
luggage—every speck—and we miss our flight—I'm
infuriated but we press on—phone ahead
to stay with my African American friend
in her beautiful four-storey home in DC—
but our taxi driver refuses to run us
to that address deep in the black part of town—I
have a dead set argument until he agrees

every corner pulsing with pimps drug dealers

hotted-up limos gunshots echoing at night

according to a recent survey this is the

most dangerous suburban street on the planet!

but neighbours greet us warmly each morning as we

hike to central DC with the Covered Wagon

we love the place but hear that since our time there the

area's been gentrified *black people forced out*

our most remarkable journey takes us to New

Orleans—we discover Amtrak—love the train trips—

comfortable seats computer games for the kids

no more plane abuse

on arrival the hotel

upgrades us to a luxurious PENTHOUSE SUITE

kids in one bedroom/Jack and I in another/

with a DOOR some romance at last! in the foyer

I find flyers on a new law legalising

twenty-four hour marriage I zoom back to our room

propose ASAP *Jack will you marry me?*

Yes I will!—there are literally dozens of

evil-looking chapels to choose from—all locked-up

like a war zone—we make arrangements for the next

day—it's wild

the celebrant's a giant of a

man/Ganur the photographer/Kaiyu quiet

in a pew but Kirrin erupts so we hold him

the whole time CHAOS! later we fine dine at a

restaurant on Bourbon Street then to bed set our

alarm and catch the train at eleven pm

Hurricane Katrina strikes immediately

after—well who knew

we're the *very* last train out

waterways are exploding—black American

families fill the cars—we travel through night and
day—hours on end—with absolutely no warning—
it's not until we reach DC that we see on
tv the disaster we've narrowly escaped

           HOW LUCKY! on our return to Australia
           Jack receives overtures from Newcastle to lead
           the Institute of Aboriginal Studies
           it's not really surprising he is THE foremost
           indigenous historian in the country
I say No—we love our life in Adelaide but
community members and colleagues urge me to
reconsider—and promotion to professor
is a significant wage leap—Mum and Dad live
in Newcastle—I'm a Worimi man so that's
my country

           my parents live close by on the North
           Coast *family contact* pulls us home I apply
           for a job in the history department and
           succeed but it's FIVE LONG MONTHS to formalise the
           contract *a drawn-out stifling time* we're STUCK in a
           caravan park staying in Jack's Winnebago
           five of us squashed with toys underfoot JACK LOVES IT!
it's terrific—fitted out with kitchen toilet
shower—my trusty home when we first meet—I build
plastic gates so the babies have their own front yard
with ride-ons—I write during the day—afternoons
three of us nap in the top bunk breeze blowing soft—
an idyllic time for me and the little blokes

           I love walking on the beach after work tiny
           ones toddling along but when will it ever end?
           I CAN'T give notice at work CAN'T organise our
           move until approval FINALLY comes then we

stay with Jack's mum eventually buy this place
which is promptly *destroyed* in yet another storm
the Pasha Bulker batters us in two thousand
and seven—bulk coal carrier runs aground on
Nobbys Beach in Newcastle during this awful
cataclysmic day—we had recently purchased
our house but had not unpacked

        NO NO when Jack says
        WE he means HE is away when it comes time to
        move and *I* pack up ALL our belongings and shift
        interstate/three kids/absent husband/then leave for
        an overseas conference boxes still piled high
        in the garage *Mum minds the kids till you return*

so here I am in our perfect new home when it
begins to rain with savage intensity—winds
violent unlike anything I've ever heard—
a river starts pouring through the door—Bloody Hell!
backyard a lake up to my knees—how can I save
two babies and a twelve-year-old—how?—power's out
we have no heating—we're marooned in the bedroom
water lapping the bed—I call the police but
they can't get through with flooding raging all over
Newcastle—Kirrin vomits I try to calm the
crying boys but I am frightened to death—this is
the longest night of my life—by morning the storm
recedes slightly I carry all three out to the
Winnebago—miraculously the engine
starts and we escape—

        Jack's email is brief Don't know
        how to tell you but OUR HOUSE IS A WRECK! I'm at
        work in Tempe Arizona and can't fathom
        what's happened ALL the phone lines are down when I get

through I'm relieved and *desperate to fly back home*
but Jack is insistent DON'T COME it's pointless now—
we're all bunked in at my parent's place—it's high up
and dry—uncles aunties sleeping on the floor no
hot water no electricity—nothing you
can do right now just work on
                    so far away and
                    feeling guilty for being a BAD MOTHER while
                    you endure this life threatening experience
I contact the Commonwealth Bank—Yes we'll send an
Assessor straight away—all our furniture cars
electricals ruined and hundreds of boxes
in the garage water-logged—How terrible the
Assessor exclaims I am writing you a cheque
for sixty thousand dollars right now!—What's this for?
We borrowed more than four hundred thousand—Oh you
didn't read the fine print he says—You're not insured
for flash floods—I'm usually a calm person
but I throw him out—contact our Labor Member
who alerts Parliament and the ABC that
Newcastle residents are being shafted by
insurance companies—I'm interviewed as well—
absolutely unleash my fury how dare they?
the ABC calls shortly after to say the
Commonwealth will pay everybody
                    but all those
                    people who accept cheques are prohibited from
                    further assistance WHAT A RACKET! we're out of
                    home for a year but *love it here* our house is quite
                    small we're around each other all the time if we
                    want to speak to one of the kids we RAISE OUR VOICE
                    lots of thumping on walls at night to quiet down
                    certain individuals *can be annoying*

the norm for most middle-class families is to
inhabit large spaces—we don't like that set up
we prefer intimacy—you know homeliness

> Jack and I have shared this study for thirteen years
> working side by side but recently we built a
> granny flat in the backyard adjacent to our
> library *soon* I'll have A ROOM OF MY OWN for
> writing! I've prayed for this since I was a child! BLISS!

our lives are enriched by writing—we have a large
grant with four indigenous researchers on the
New South Wales Aborigines Protection Board—
it's unique as Katie's the only whitefella—
most often it's one token blackfella and a
crateload of white profs—Katie and I love to play
with various concepts—sometimes publish jointly

Sex, Race and Power
Aboriginal Men and White Women in Australian History

Nearly every recent history of Aboriginal peoples in Australia makes some reference to relationships between Aboriginal women and white men, but virtually none mentions the inverse relationship between Aboriginal men and white women. The present paper examines these historically obscured and erased interracial relationships. These relationships represent a myriad of experiences, any study of sex and love across racial boundaries being a revelation of devotion, fear, triumph and pain, as well as of broader cultural and gender issues, legal and political struggles. A collaborative methodology and approach recognises the significance of race and gender perspectives in researching and writing interracial history. [*Australian Historical Studies* 126, 2005]

> I'm very pregnant when we present this paper
> white woman/Aboriginal man arguing
> the importance of re-writing history from
> both sides of the fence *quite hilarious* telling

our audience how ardently committed we
are *body and mind* to this research agenda
we really have fun I'm so INSPIRED working with
Jack our intellect and passions fully aligned
passion for Aboriginal history and
for each other—our household possesses the most
extensive library on indigenous rights
on the planet—honestly every room is
bursting with documents and books—we adore it!
but life's fragile you give us an ENORMOUS scare
you always go overseas when disaster hits!
I'm on my way to Sydney to give a talk—send
the boys off to high school when suddenly I feel
this pain across my jaw and heaviness in the
chest—Doctor Google says Potential Heart Attack!
I stop at Emergency hoping I can get
to Sydney on time but the ECG says No—
one artery is ninety per cent blocked
we're SHOCKED!
heart attack stent recovery brings home the vast
age gap between us *I never worried before*
one day Katie will be on her own—
my whole life
entwined with yours/our research our romance our boys
how can it *possibly* be any other way?
for now we're strong—as always we adapt and move
on to the next challenge—and the next—together

Luis and Barney

Just one week after being introduced to one another, Luis and Barney become a couple—Luis is twenty-nine, Barney thirty-two. During their forty-four years together they endure arduous periods of illness and hospitalisation, but never waver in their commitment to one another. Now retired, Barney's career was in student counselling, and he was later Director of the International Student Centre at a prominent university. Luis reinvented himself time and again after each illness—from engineer to restaurateur to caterer to interior designer. Food has always been central to their lives, entertaining with geniality, generosity and flair. On February 9, 2018, Luis and Barney marry in their Woollahra garden, surrounded by family and friends. As theirs is one of the earliest gay marriages in Sydney following the passage of the Marriage Equality Law in Australia in late 2017, the joyful proceedings are filmed and later aired by the BBC.

Luis

This moment we meet—Surry Hills nineteen seventy-four. A
mutual friend invites us to champagne brunch. When I arrive
two Barneys are present—both bearded, both psychologists, one

Aussie, one South African. Both fancy me. So I'm darting
between them—from kitchen to lounge to kitchen, but only one
Barney persists. He is shy, a striking face, acute blue eyes—

not aware of his beauty. I do enjoy making him blush.
He's lovely so I say Why don't you come to my house tonight?
I'm having a few people. A superb time. I show off by

throwing fruit up in the air and setting it alight. Sparks are
flying everywhere but I hold him off that first night. I feel
uneasy. He's like a Mack truck without brakes, moving fast. This

is our beginning—illness pushes us to pledge our love. My
brain is haemorrhaging. I'm so sick I may die. Doctors tell
me to advise family—my chances of surviving are

very poor. I make a will and organise my funeral.
The day I finally leave hospital is Barney's birthday.
I'm weak, emaciated. The world looks grim. I write a note:

I do not have a present for you, all I can offer is
forty-five kilos of love. Will you want me and love me now?
His being lights up. He is incandescent! Yes he says. I

will never leave you—*hasta el cielo, las estrellas*
y el infinito—my love as vast as the sky, the stars
and infinity. This vow forged in fire and grief connects us

ever after—the moment when Barney and I unite for
life. So many years ago—yet he has always been my light.
He illuminates my path. There will be no me without him.

Barney

Luis works for Nestlé as an engineer. His hair smells of
chocolate, his clothing too—my sweetie. I'm thrilled he asks
me to dinner, but when I arrive nobody's home. How strange.

After twenty minutes a young woman appears. She eyes me
suspiciously as if I'm loitering, slams the door shut,
interrogates me through the peep-hole. Who are you and how do

you know Luis? Why are you here? What was he wearing at brunch
this morning? I'm terribly confused. It's clear this woman lives
with him. Did I imagine the earlier flirtation? Then

in sweeps Luis, bags bursting with groceries, two friends in tow.
He cooks one of his 'simple little' dinners—magnificence
in a moment. I'm seduced, warmed by rich conversation and

brilliant food. But suddenly I remember my promise to
fetch a mate from the airport. I don't want to leave but Luis
says Come back for desert if it's not too late. He waits for me—

his exotic *crêpes flambées* are breathtaking. I'm bursting with
hope for further 'sweets' to come. Luis asks if I'll kindly drive
his friends home. They have to catch an early plane. Thus I'm despatched.

Crestfallen, I persevere. A week later I ask him to
dinner at my apartment in Bronte. I roast a leg of
lamb. On the balcony we chat—a startling blue moon, our hands

touch lightly. We move inside, becoming closer. Luis turns
off the oven. We wake at three, starving, leg of lamb waiting
all this time. Delicious. Next morning we ring in sick, spend the

day at Jenolan Caves. I won't leave his side again. I love
his Latin hauteur. His self-confidence is enticing to
the diffident young man I am then. We're so different. He's

frank and forthright, always right. I'm discreet and diplomatic,
more subtle. Yet when Luis and I connect, I burst out of
the closet and embrace life. There will be no me without him.

Luis

I have always been close to my mother and sisters. The day
after my brain surgery, my eldest sister Marta flies
from Chile to Australia on a compassion visa.

Such a sad reunion! I am a ghost with holes in my head,
bandages wrapped like a turban! The nurse puts blush on my cheeks
so I won't frighten my Marta. When Barney takes her home to

our place in Bondi she asks Where will Luiso sleep? He won't
tell her about our relationship—he doesn't dare to say.
So I ask our dear friend Sofia to reveal everything!

It's trying at first, quite emotional. *Mi familia*
know me as a man who loves women—for eight years I was with
Sofia's sister! I'm so sick by December *mi madre*

sells her house in Chile and arrives with my sister Lola.
I won't let him die she says, without me. She just comes. Our life
becomes one operation after another. It takes ten

years to resolve! Nena stays with us eighteen months—my sisters
tambien, until we buy them a lovely apartment in
Matraville. Nena is forever thankful to Barney and

aware of the sacrifices he makes to accommodate
me—keep me alive. Nena respects that. Calls him *mi otro
hijo*—my other son. She knows there is no me without him.

Barney

My parents don't know I'm gay. There have been women in my life,
but no men. I tell them all about Luis, they perceive he's
a significant person to me, but nothing is ever

said until they ask us to their house on the Central Coast for
the weekend. My stepfather, whom I always thought terribly
homophobic says You'll be able to see the lake in the

morning. I've moved the double bed into the spare room. That is
the only acknowledgement. My mum Lorna adores Luis.
She's a self-sacrificing woman. Luis brings glamour to

her life—cuts her hair, applies make-up and spoils her with special
extravagances. She is delighted that I'm happy and
settled at last, grateful for his devotion to me. The first

time my parents visit us in Sydney, Luis enchants with
a 'simple little' Sunday lunch—fillet of beef perfectly
rare, exquisite chargrilled prawns, pink grapefruit salad. For dessert

he creates a rockmelon boat, floating on a sea of green
jelly, fruit skewers for sails. Amazing! He wins them over
completely. In time, they will see there is no me without him.

Celebrant

Welcome friends. For Luis and Barney the Same Sex Marriage Act
brings decades of waiting to an end. Today they will be joined
before the eyes of the law. Luis and Barney betrothed just

one week after they met—when homosexuality was
still illegal all across Australia. Yet another
ten years passed until it was decriminalised in New South

Wales. Clearly their union is testament to the power of
loving gay relationships. Luis and Barney have not rushed
into marriage—but on this tenth day of February, two

thousand and eighteen, their love is finally legal. So by
the authority vested in me and after forty-four
years together, I declare them to be husband and husband.

Barney

Why should we marry now? We betrothed long ago in private,
it's enough. But Luis insists. Finally we are free to
make our vows public, he says—before all our family, friends

and society. We can be completely proud of who we
are. Of course he's right. To say out loud we're still here, closer than
ever. It's an achievement. So many times I almost lose

him, yet he keeps going. He's so bloody strong and determined—
and so devoted to my needs. Illness has complicated
life, but also confirmed we can't be one without the other.

Luis

We are overwhelmed by the joy of our nieces, nephews and
all the young men who have loved us as fathers over many
years. *Fabuloso* they say! At last you can now marry! Our

lives have been rich—travelling the world, entertaining our friends,
creating homes and gardens we love. But six years ago he
almost dies after bypass surgery. Cardiac arrest

twice. ICU forty-two days. Our friend Walter even gives
him last rites! Doctors believe I bring him out of the coma.
Barney's refusing food—pulls out his tubes. I make chicken soup—

dab tiny drops with cotton wool. He licks his lips, then his mouth
opens just a little so I can nourish him with the warm
broth. Recovery is drawn out, but he comes back to me. I

prepare lunch and dinner each day, spoil him rotten. My reward
is to look after him now. For nearly half a century
he's been there—enduring my persistent poor health—accepting

all the risks. Life has not been always easy for us but we
survive, more intimate than ever. When life's fragile what else
can you do but give love? *No hay yo sin él. No hay él sin mí.*

Nick and Elena

Nick and Elena's paths initially cross at a church dance in Melbourne on March 25th, 1992. Elena, aged twenty, is totally disinterested in Greek men, but the young blond Nick, aged twenty-one, doesn't look Greek at all. Yet their secretive dating, and subsequent courtship, betrothal and marriage are steeped in the traditions of Greek culture. They speak quickly and with laughter as they detail the tensions they juggle—honouring their own values while trying to accommodate the expectations of the extended Greek family. They champion each other's careers—Nick with Victoria Police and Elena as CEO of a not-for-profit that supports women, girls and families. Over time they have developed skilled teamwork, raising two sons while also satisfying the demands of an ever-fluid schedule of work and travel. Their home in Northcote is the epicentre of frequent celebrations—Easter, birthdays, weddings, baptisms. We speak at their kitchen table on a Sunday morning, accompanied by generous platters of feta cheese, tomatoes from their lush garden and yellow peppers marinated by Nick.

Nick

We first meet on Greek Independence Day. My youth group in Brunswick
and Elena's in Preston combine with other churches for a
huge community dance. We're dressed in our regional costumes—mine
from Crete and Elena's from Macedonia. Comes down to fate

really. So much history between us—neither area seen
as part of the 'real' Greece. Following four hundred years of Turkish
occupation when independence is finally won, Crete and
Macedonia are left out—forgotten. We help each other

[we do]. It's Venizelos—the revered leader from Crete who helps
secure freedom for Macedonia in the Balkan Wars. My
baba often talks of the historic connection—Elena's
grandmother has a profound affection and respect for Cretans.

Elena

My great-great-grandfather Ilias was a freedom fighter—the
last of five priests in our family line—teaching Greek in secret
to keep language alive during Turkish rule. Macedonia
doesn't gain independence until nineteen twenty-one *[that's' right]*.

I'm raised in the traditional Greek way—my grandparents share our
house, my auntie across the road. I'm the eldest, the only girl
so the pressure's on to attend Greek functions—I don't like Greek men
[no you don't!] excluding my dad of course—a gentle beautiful

man. The boys I grow up with are completely macho. I'll never
marry a Greek bloke, I swear! But there I am at the Preston Hall
because our youth group is hosting the dance. I open the door, turn
to my best friend and say As if I'll meet anyone here. Then *Bham!*

There he is! Nick. Collecting tickets from people—very handsome.
He doesn't look Grecian—blond hair and freckles. Oh my God, they have
an Aussie here in Greek costume! I can't stop looking at him. We
dance—traditional *horos* of every kind. The spark is lit.

Nick

I'm incredibly attracted to Elena from the moment
we meet, but I'm shy. I join the same church group committees to be
near her. Our first date is coffee on Lygon Street but secretly—
no-one can know. I bring flowers—find more excuses to see her.

No social media then. Sometimes we talk for hours on the phone.
Me manoeuvring the stretchy cord from kitchen to laundry in
order to speak in private [*Yia Yia yelling Who's on the phone?*]. I'm
head over heels—totally besotted after only three months.

Elena

It's a big deal being first-born—meet the right man, make something of
your life—huge expectations. Nick quickly decides we're perfect, but
I struggle—still determined to put career first and not marry
Greek. Dad comes from grinding poverty, though his father was mayor

of Parori—their village in Greece. The Germans confiscated
their dwelling during the second world war—shoved them into stables
with the animals—later their house burnt down *[twice!]* . Dad migrates here
with absolutely nothing—settles in Koo Wee Rupp—runs a fish

and chips shop at first, then a deli—in Greece he was a tailor.
Eventually he starts men's clothing manufacture with two
Greek business partners. Extraordinary achievement. So Nick
enters a high-pressure context—what will he achieve with *his* life?

Nick

So nerve-wracking to meet Elena's mum and dad. I'm training as
an officer at the Military College up in Duntroon
but drop out—work with my father in his small cabinet-making
company, while thinking to join the police. Elena's worried—

this guy she's introducing has no job—I won't measure up. I
bring flowers and sweets—they're waiting at the door. *Yassas!* Sit in the
middle! Now what will you make of yourself? I'm sweating profusely
but I swiftly connect to Yia Yia, the matriarch—*[he charms her*

completely]. If you get past her you're in! My parents are much less
demanding. Baba is one of seven siblings, but arrives in
Australia in the sixties on his own. I'll be back in a
few years, he says. Don't come. But he decides to stay—organises

to bring a bride from a nearby village in Crete—through letters and
photos they arrange a marriage. Mama's only seventeen but
keen to get away. They're married now for fifty-three years. Mine's a
small close-knit family—they support whatever I want to do.

Elena

I am completely beside myself—don't appreciate this group
inquisition of Nick—everyone full-on, way too invested.
Growing up as a female in this so-Greek space is difficult.
I fight with my parents about university—about who

I'll marry. I'm strong-willed but learn to work the system—cajole my
brother Stavros to advocate behind the scenes. No need. Nick is
so poised and elegant—he captivates them all! Oh my God, they
say. Such a *kýrios!* They adore him ever since. One gate down—

onto the next *[the families meet]*. Greeks call it *Logos*—the groom
and his parents are invited to the bride's home to honour his
word that they will marry. This custom pushes me too far—as if
I'm a chattel to be bartered over. I'm a feminist—this

is not for me! But it's tricky, as Nick's parents embrace *Logos*
as well. I fight very hard. In the end we do not exchange rings
and call it an *Introduction* instead. Small difference perhaps
but my whole life I endure such practices. Not any longer!

Nick

Some traditions we love. Like *Kolak*. The night before the wedding,
a function at Elena's house for over a hundred people.
Traditional music, dancing—a Macedonian on the
clarinet. I bring a few Cretan musicians *[Yia Yia's over*

the moon]. As my relatives arrive we're greeted at the front door.
Yia Yia hands out charming towels she's crocheted especially for all
the men—beautiful aprons for the women. Theios holds a bowl
of flour which he dabs on our faces—wishing us long life. Our dads

break the *kolak* together. We all take a piece and dance with the
bread—it's wonderful. Two weeks before we have *Krevati* at our
house. The bridal bed is pressed and strewn with flowers and everyone
places money on the bed—for good fortune and prosperity.

Elena

They want the wedding at a Greek Reception Centre. We say No!
We marry at St Kilda Town Hall—November nineteen ninety-
six—three hundred and fifty guests *[initially her mum wanted*
five hundred!]. We try to carve out our own space—manage the tensions.

But even our house is a massive issue. You're buying an old
weatherboard in Northcote? Come to Epping! Buy brand new! A constant
battle—what they want—what we need—compromise. It creates a firm
foundation for Nick and I to negotiate the pressures in

our lives. We operate like a military exercise with
everyday contingencies—never certain what's coming next. We
must be agile—communicate, deal with multiple stresses—get
good jobs, pay off the mortgage, guide the kids—keep everyone content.

Nick

Baba often talks in parables—he says a relationship
is like holding two ends of a rope—you need give and take. If you're
both pulling tight, it's a standoff—you have to let up *[give some slack]*.
I know it's simplistic but it's always in the back of my mind—

that image of the rope. We live by *filótimo*—some call it
the Greek secret. No English word translates. It's a combination
of one's virtue and moral obligation—knowing the right thing,
the wrong thing—being compassionate and fair. It's deeply ingrained—

a concept we've both grown up with. If a person is unjust to
another we say Hey where's your *filótimo?* But some aspects
of our culture are wrong—like chauvinism *[absolutely]*. Men
up here, women below. We're not like that. From the outset I know

Elena's a strong woman—smarter than me, very wise. All the
aunts/uncles/cousins seek her advice. When a new career move comes
her way I say Go for it. Awesome. Old-style men from Crete would say
No. I'm super proud of her achievements, I'd never hold her back.

Elena

I see how rare he is immediately—nothing like the Greek
guys I'm running from. Nick's tender, respectful, clever. I was a
corrections officer for six years, so I grasp the violent
world of Nick's job—removing children from mothers, seeing folk on

the worst day of their lives. It's traumatic for police. When Nick comes
home he absolutely needs time to debrief. Our work can be so
confronting, challenging—but a gift, giving us purpose, focus.
Don't sweat the small stuff! Appreciate what we have! Find our balance!

Above all I respect how Nick deals with the racism against
him—Greeks never promoted in the ranks *[wogs!]*. But he stays true to
his integrity despite enormous pressure. Sergeants goad him
because he refuses brutality in the cells, advocates

change—threatens the status quo. This kind gentle man—the type VicPol
clearly needs—stressed out, undermined throughout his career *[for twenty
years!]*. Thankfully the force changes at last—officers like Nick now
recognised and promoted. As a Supervisor, his shift work

is insane. Rarely do we know the timetable two weeks out. Yet
oddly it breaks up the mundane—provides us with days to ourselves—
freedom to grow personally while raising our boys—enough time
to meet the obligations and demands of our loving Greek tribe.

Nick

I love what I do. But a huge culture shock in the early years!
Colleagues say Look out Nick! Soon you'll become a drinker, a smoker,
a womaniser *[they do but you don't!]*. When night shift ends it's off
to early openers—guzzling steins of beer at six am. Are

you kidding me? Serious? What's wrong with these people? I'm never
going to do that. At times I want to quit, transfer to teaching—
and eventually that's what I do. Being Supervisor
I guide our new, young constables *[they love him]*—induct them into

good values—introduce new ideas for consideration.
I carry out my job in a nurturing way. I don't mean to
brag but my approach is widely acknowledged by my peers. I'm proud.
And I have more leave. Recently we took our two boys to Greece for

the first time. Visiting our parents' villages was profound. In
Kato Kleines, Elena's uncle brings us to the house where her
mum was raised—it's half a shack now—at one time forty people crammed
inside. Witnessing such hardship makes it painfully real for us.

Elena

In Parori, we visit Baba's old house. We're blown away. In
the bedroom occupied by Germans we see Yia Yia's writing on
the wall—*Kaló Pascha!* Happy Easter! Determined to make her
mark before her entire family is evacuated. We

find her paintbrush on the floor—my God—those words still radiating
after all these years. We source original entry documents
for both sets of grandparents, but many records have been destroyed
or lost—it's gut-wrenching. We do discover the signature of

the priest who married Yia Yia—her grandfather! Our heritage comes
alive for the boys in a way I never appreciated
when I was young. But history's vulnerable. Will our grandkids
speak Greek or know their culture? Yia Yia gifted me her grandfather's

liturgy book. Inside she's catalogued our family saga—
songs from weddings and funerals. Her final words. Tell the tale of
our ancestors to your brothers, your children, so they remember
who we are. Where we come from. Goodness! *[no pressure]*. Of course we will …

Imogen and Luc

Unlike the other couples in this book, Imogen and Luc have been married for only four years, yet they have been together in heart and mind for twenty. They fall in love in Queensland in 2002, when Imogen is twenty, Luc twenty-three. After an intense seven months in Cairns, they go their separate ways and become involved in other relationships. While they keep in contact as friends and email confidantes, their unrequited/unacknowledged passion simmers. Their joy and elation as they recall being reunited in 2017 is extraordinarily contagious. They share a love of people and a fascination with each other and the world. Luc has chosen a career in words and translation to allow him to land in any number of places. Imogen's lifetime commitment to social issues sees her working to develop innovative programs at the nexus of the health and criminal justice systems. They live in Melbourne where they marry in 2018.

Imogen

I'm sick as a dog with flu, living in an apartment block
called Blue Sail Court—hideous egg-shell blue with a massive fish
out front and kidney-shaped pool—tackiest place you've ever seen.

My bestie Debbie insists I get some sun. I drag an old
mattress to the pool in my sarong/singlet/sunglasses and
fall asleep. Strange sounds arouse me—a deep toffee British voice

bearing down on me asking what the block is like—and a soft
French accent—this turns out to be Luc. Debbie hosts a welcome
barbecue when he moves in. We speak all night long. I'm smitten.

Luc

The first time I leave Canada I'm eighteen, out to explore
le monde—Europe, the Middle East, Asia, home to Quebec then
off again. I'm addicted to travel. I'm not sure what to

study or what to do in life. It's easy finding work here
and there in hospitality. When I hear about the one-
year working holiday visa for Australia I say

That's for me. *C'est parfait.* I start in Melbourne, but after six
months the cold drives me north to Cairns. My neighbour is Imogen.
We start dating straight away. It's really weird. It just happens.

Imogen

We are inseparable. Luc works eighty hours a week, crawls
into bed, we share breakfast or dinner and he's out again.
I'm employed at the small IGA market across the road.

This is my Gap Year—it lasts thirty-six months! After year twelve
I'm adrift, a bit lost, and fall into a dysfunctional
relationship with an older guy. My godmother helps me

escape to Bundaberg, but I hate life there so when Debbie
visits we fly off to Cairns. It's cleansing. And when I meet Luc
life is wonderful, but he's always about *I'm leaving soon,*

don't get attached. I'm afraid. It's hard for me. I know we're in
love, but the end point dangles—an imminent split always in
the air. And soon I'll return home to start university.

Luc

We're young. Not really ready to settle down. Imogen's just
twenty—she escapes Tassie to get her bearings, I escape
through travel. I like the life. It actually takes ten months

to get home—through Malaysia, Thailand, Egypt. I hitch-hike
from Cairo to Istanbul, tour Syria at the end of
the Gulf War, fly to Belgium, France. But before I leave Debbie

suggests I surprise Imogen for Christmas. Why not? I'd love
to but I'm torn. Her life is here, mine will be there. How can I
say *non*? My head says one thing, my heart another. The heart wins.

Imogen

Still my favourite memory of all time. I'm in a pub
in Launceston with my friends. I feel someone tickling my ears.
I'm annoyed. Who is that? I turn around and Oh My God you're

here!! I scream and jump into Luc's arms. An amazing two weeks!
He meets my whole family—makes a special connection with
my Irish granddad who speaks with him in Gaelic. Then it ends.

I'm gutted. Half-way down the tarmac he bolts back to kiss me.
I'm inconsolable, sobbing, but we stay in touch. I keep
every single email he writes, sixteen years of missives

squished into a tiny box he sends from Egypt. I begin
university in Hobart, living with my brother. His
mate Sam asks me out. I've known him since we were fourteen. I say

Nope I'm still in love with Luc. But it's clear he won't be back—he's
enrolled in translation studies at Quebec Uni. I'm heart-
broken but my rational mind kicks in. I have to move on.

Luc

*Hey there beautiful! Thank you for telling me what you think, not
what you believe I want to hear. It is difficult to let
go. Your feelings for Sam will take time to surface because our*

*connection is still so strong and I'd be a fool to ruin
my prospects in Quebec. As time goes by it's obvious we
are living an impossible love. We need to exit this*

*grey area soon. I know this emptiness will last a while,
but the heart will calm down, won't it? Eventually. You make
me smile, my love. Email me back at my new address. Huge hugs.*

Imogen

Sam's studying law, I'm doing social work. Our lives are on
track, intertwined. We're doing fine. After we graduate it's
off to Melbourne for a challenging job. We love each other but

not the rapture I've known with Luc. In time Sam wants kids, a house,
combined incomes. I resist. We persevere. I'm travelling
to New York for a forum in two thousand and nine. Quebec's

not far away so I arrange to stay for a week with Luc
and his girlfriend Chloe. What am I thinking? Is he madly
in love with her? What do I wear? I remember arriving

at Montreal Airport—completely focused on hugging her.
Go to the girlfriend first. She's from France—we double kiss, Luc hugs
me. Okay this will be fine, I think. Fine. That first night I'm wedged

on the sofa between them, charged by magnetic tension I
don't understand. Each day I explore the city, Chloe goes
to the lab—she's a biochemist—and Luc translates from home.

Third day is bloody hot. I return mid-afternoon, shower,
collapse on the chair in his study, legs resting on the wall.
He's typing and suddenly stops. It's weird isn't it? I swing

around. What? I still feel it. *Je t'adore*. It's so hard to have
you in my house. Oh My God! I love him, of course, but I have
a partner and so does he—we can't do a thing about it.

The last four days are torture. Nightmare drive to the airport, she's
in the back seat, my stomach aching, Luc feels ill—them walking
away—he glances at me over his shoulder, disappears.

Luc

Finally we talk about the elephant in the room. We
trace over our long history—everything that's happened since
meeting in Cairns—Chloe and I three years, she and Sam seven.

We have to stick with *raison*. But talking openly is so
explosif—it dissolves all barriers. I don't know what I'm
hoping. *J'adore* Chloe. But the connection with Imogen

consumes me. I want the truth. And after she returns to
Australia and breaks up with Sam, it goes straight to my guts.
She actually does it! Do I do the same? Take a leap

of faith? I say *Non. Ma vie est dans Quebec.* My translating
work can follow me anywhere so that's no excuse, but friends,
the city, I'm building my roots here. And I feel uneasy

to love two women, it's not right. I need to decide and stand
by it. Head and heart in struggle again. With distance the head
takes over yet I never stop loving Imogen. *Jamais.*

Narrator

Don't worry, nothing's over yet! FYI Luc stays with his
Chloe seven more years, glued at the hip. Imogen doesn't
date, throws herself completely into work—twelve-hour days wrestling

wily bureaucrats and government agencies. She's exhausted—
no room for anyone else! But colleagues conspire to create
her profile on EHarmony. She's horrified. First man she

meets is Drew. Fast forward four years. Their passion is politics,
social action, the Greens. The relationship is loving but
always volatile, a struggle. Imogen ignores the signs.

They buy a house together, get engaged—travel overseas
in two thousand and seventeen. A crazy plan is hatched— they'll
meet up with Luc and Chloe in Berlin. Do they believe in

fate? The rendezvous fails. Luc's plane struck by lightning in Toulouse.
Mon Dieu! They arrive one day (too) late. Imogen flies to Prague,
Drew to Australia. Luc takes the bus to Prague. Watch closely!

Imogen

I'm waiting in my hotel off Wenceslas Square, writing notes
for my presentation. Suddenly he's on the stairs. I see
his perfect reflection in the mirror. So lovely. He wants

to attend my forum's opening event. The symphony
is gorgeous. I feel his body beside me, his eyes on me.
We have three days to enjoy Prague. When he leaves I'll box it up—

already I'm preparing for sadness. But we have such fun—
I don't attend many sessions. The night he leaves in tears, heart
wavering, I lawyer up, rationalise our decision.

At home, things disintegrate with Drew. I don't sleep in our bed,
we're back in couples therapy—then we break absolutely.
I email all night with Luc. I wait until he is awake—

ten at night here—we speak until he insists I go to sleep,
talk again at five. Back/and/forth—unfulfilled love for so long.
Is he sure it's real? I know how logical he likes to be.

Luc

Hypocrisy is wrong. How many years do I stay true to
Chloe, yet find I'm still in love with Imogen. *Le courage*
to finally leave—I'm so relieved, over the moon, certain

I've done the right thing. For Imogen's birthday I send twenty
jars of apple butter—her favourite—and scan a copy
of my airline ticket—Montreal to Melbourne November

eighth one-way. She finds an apartment in her brother's building
so I have family connection. A welcome gift awaits
me: Nesquik—I love hot chocolate, a myki card, mobile

phone, a small speaker as I suffer from tinnitus. Photos
decorate the fridge—us in Prague, me and my friends in Quebec,
brand new furniture from IKEA. She does it all—builds a

nest for us at lightening speed. She's amazing! At the airport
my flight is delayed. We wait. Wait. Wait. Then I'm leaping over
the barrier, she's running parallel screaming LUC! At last.

Imogen

It actually happens—we're together now a whole year!
Body, heart and mind finally aligned. We're invited on
a five-day cruise from Sydney to Cairns with seventeen of my

family members to celebrate Grandma's eightieth. It
takes five days to get there, but Luc's glad for time to break into
my tight Irish clan. For his fortieth birthday we party

in Cairns. At Christmas time we're off to Canada so I can
meet his family. What a whirlwind. Our wedding is May twelfth
two thousand and eighteen. The ceremony is intimate,

only our closest people attend. Afterwards a no-fuss
wine and cheese at our local trendy bar in Brunswick. We're still
amazed by the everyday ease. Luc is now free to do his own

thing and not feel guilty. If I'm working late or caught up in
difficult demands, there's no criticism. Don't worry, Luc
says, You're exhausted we'll have an early night. He wants to care

for me. Who knew relationships were meant to be stress-free? From
time to time though, I still stop and stare at him in disbelief.
You're here Luc! And he smiles. *Je suis ici.* I am here with you.

About the Author

Barbara Kamler is a Melbourne poet and Emeritus Professor of Education at Deakin University. She arrived in Australia as a young teacher in the early 70s and developed a distinguished academic career over the next forty years. She is the author or editor of nine academic books and over sixty journal articles and book chapters on literacy, writing pedagogy and identity. Her debut poetry collection *Leaving New Jersey* (2016) is a memoir of fifty-six prose poems, recounting the story of leaving America and of arriving in Australia—an artful tale of putting down roots and tearing them up in one woman's quest for home. Her poetry has appeared in publications such as *The Age, The Australian, Australian Poetry Journal, Poetrix, Poetry New Zealand*, as well as various anthologies. 'The usual questions do not pertain' was shortlisted for the 2017 Newcastle Poetry Prize. *Two tales of long love* (2019) is a chapbook precursor to this volume, celebrating two couples who sustain love over many years, despite the vagaries of life that intervene.

Lightning Source UK Ltd.
Milton Keynes UK
UKHW010955200522
403294UK00004BA/369

9 781925 736489